108 Timeless Truths for Peaceful and Joyful Living

એક વખત ના પ્રાર્થના જય જય સૌ ને!   June 2004

"A BEAUTIFIC PRESENTATION OF DADA'S COSMO VISION"

With the quiet, gentle blessings, guidance & support of her Godfather, Shri GA Shah; Mahatma & Sanghpati Worldwide for Jay Sachchidanand Sangh, Shaila Mulji, through Dada's divine grace has produced a rendering of English translation meticulously collected and parceled, in 108 caplets, originally composed by Mahatma Varya Shri Jasubhai Shah, the divine vision of Shri Dada Bhagavan, with her reflective flashes would hopefully serve as a reference book to the aspiring souls for a happy, harmonious life leading to liberation. Her reflective flashes are direct & piercing as though she was thinking out loud helping the inquisitive ones to see within and seek the solution to their problems. A painstaking self endeavor to shed light on the path of permanent peace and bliss.

On behalf of Jay Sachchidanand Sangh, we heartily welcome this beautific presentation of Shaila Mulji with her will to help people discover their inner strength and confront & combat their challenges & crises; and ultimately make their life worth living freely & fearlessly.

With Blessings,

Kanudadaji.

9th June '04

Shri Kanudadaji i Jai Sat-chit-Anand.

જય સચ્ચિદાનંદ

1.∞

108 Timeless Truths for Peaceful and Joyful Living
Based on the Science of Absolutism
A unique perspective on life from the inside out

Shaila Krupa Karuna

2004

108 Timeless Truths for
Peaceful and Joyful Living

Table of Contents

Author's Note

Dear Reader,

This 108 verse song/poem was originally written by a divinely inspired devotee of Kripalu Dev Shrimad Rajchandra, Jashubhai Shah, a prominent lawyer, who found a profound connection with Shri Dada Bhagavan that inspired his poetry and song. He was blessed by Shri Dada Bhagavan to give spiritual talks and traveled widely throughout the U. S., U.K. and India. His talks were soul stirring and thought provoking. Throughout his lifetime, Jashubhai Shah, even when both his legs were amputated stayed steadfast, positive and completely poised in the seat of the Pure Soul. Even today, when he is no longer with us physically, his poetry sings the glory of eternity.
This translation cannot do justice to the purity, profoundness and simplicity of his words... however, is an attempt to transfer the essence of each verse. This is written to help you get through the trials and tribulations of this chaotic, clash-filled and bitter age. Also to enable you to look within for the answers and riches that lay dormant within you. If you have taken 'knowledge' from the Absolute Scientist, this will be easier to understand. However, if you have not, it is ideal if the desire to know your eternal Pure Soul is ignited and the ardent desire to meet a 'Gyani Purush' is manifested. That is my goal dear reader for you.

Please forgive me in advance for any misunderstanding that may occur due to translation errors and the limitations of the English language.

With utmost humility, reverence and undivided devotion to the Gyani Purush, Shri Dada Bhagavan,

Shaila Krupa Karuna

Verse #1

"In the workings of nature, there is no such thing as injustice, dear soul!
Look not for justice or injustice...
For what has occurred and is occurring is just in itself."

ॐ

Reflective Flashes-

With the neurons and dendrites in our small minds, we attempt to make sense of the workings of the world as our opinions flip-flop like a fish out-of-water. Just when we think that we've figured it all out... something changes... a curve ball is thrown! This usually occurs on a daily basis. Therefore, judge NOT. Be open, flexible and ready for change at all times. This life is a film created by our own intentions, projections and karma, we do not need to 'see' the film of anyone but our own. Make sure your file #1 performs worldly duties, stays within the fine line of 'pure' living and discharge. Be not fearless with regards to alcohol, drugs or sex. See & know the world as a JUST place... but be vigilant and protect the Pure Soul... not the 'relative' self.

If we cannot laugh at ourselves, we have wasted our time here on earth in this age of clash & quarrel. Flashes of the past's perceived injustices continue to haunt our daily existence. Let them go... they were just part of the film. Get not engrossed in the pre-recorded film nature is playing for us... be a knower-perceiver-seer in the drama that is being played out. Take not a 'real' position in favor of anyone. It is NOT a war... in the language of the Pure Soul... we are all one. Even if we must go in the courts to settle a claim, it is all within the realm of the 'relative'. Allow nature to catch 'our' faults... it is beneficial. 'We' are free from the moment the fault has been revealed and the account has been settled.

Verse #2

"One living being has no power to disturb another; without a karmic link no one or no thing cannot obstruct another."

ॐ

Reflective Flashes—

We signed and endorsed the check to be with the present people in our lives. Our closest kin and loved ones were all endorsed 100% by us! This may have been done out of ignorance or knowledge or a combination thereof.

We wonder why it is always our little sibling who bothers us or our elder sibling who is always hogging all the attention in the family! We may wonder why we are always last priority or completely ignored? It is not worth wasting energy on these queries. This is all a pre-recorded film playing itself out now as we live our lives. The mind, body and speech are but operating on the prompts of a pre-recorded cosmic software which executes as the hardware gives the cues. Our intentions of the past are the operator of the hardware through a very subtle, powerful and impartial energy.

When someone disturbs our peace of mind, we immediately get agitated and, to top it off, we form some nasty opinions. The fact of the matter is, that entity is merely 'instrumental' in delivering the fruits of our own seeds. Our intellect will wrangle with us showing us all the horrible things this entity has done to us. The mailman has to deliver mail whether it is good news or bad. The news is our own. We must realize the people & living beings in our lives are the same. They are there as deliverers of good and bad mail depending on what we signed-up for in the past.

One of our biggest enemies on the Akram path to liberation is sensitivity. This kicks in due to the 'sticky' belief from the past that 'I' am in fact this mind, body & speech. In order to fully understand & experience being a non-doer and knower-perceiver only, it is crucial for us to be able to 'see' our closest loved ones and kin as completely innocent instruments dancing to the tune of their own past karma. When someone slaps us in the face or offers a repulsive insult, it should in fact be received as divine nectar to help remove the poison of excess and displaced ego from our 'relative' imperfect projected 'Self'. Shower those who insult, harm or throw stones at you with positive blessings and, in turn, be blessed.

Verse #3

"From the moment the realization occurs, 'I myself am the worst culprit of all'; one becomes worthy of pure, eternal knowledge."

❧

Reflective Flashes—

This is an extremely bitter pill to swallow. It will force you to purge yourself of all your excess baggage because the fingers can only point in one direction. When I met 'Dada' for the very first time, I told him, "I have committed many sins." His response to me was, "So have I." That was when I realized that I was in the presence of an extremely enlightened and great Pure Soul. He did not chastise me or tell me that I am unworthy. He validated my concern and put Himself at my level. Only a truly enlightened and 100% pure being can accomplish this! From that moment forward my 'oneness' with Him has been unbroken.

Be not afraid to stand up to the 'relative' self. It is perfectly sane and healthy to engage in 'self-talk'. Actually, in this day-and-age of clash & quarrel, it is the only way to make any progress. We cannot afford to endorse the thoughts & opinions of our 'relative' self as those were planted out of ignorance. We must work against the tide and declare a war against all those wrong beliefs we have carried with us for infinite lives.

The first and foremost is that 'I am this person.' Actually, you did not even name yourself! You had no say in the matter! How can you be this person in reality? Furthermore, if we see our own faults, they automatically will dissolve. If we catch a thief in our home, will the thief attempt to escape or not? Once we turn the inward light on, the faults are bound to be discovered and burnt to ashes by the power of the Pure Soul. If you do not provide fuel to an engine, it cannot run! Do not fuel the 'relative' self with false ego and support. Stay seated in the royal throne of the Pure Soul and remain a knower-perceiver-seer and infinite knowledge, vision, energy and bliss will be yours without fail. Let all the dirty water backed-up in your karmic pipes exhaust itself!

Verse #4

"Through the web of karmic links all living beings come together, as that karmic link dissolves, the parting also occurs... In the absence of the 'karmic link', nothing occurs."

ॐ

Reflective Flashes—

One man's trash is another man's treasure! Your karmic link with an individual may be bound by caustic and spiteful intentions on both sides. In this instance, this relationship, on the surface, seems to be one of pain & suffering. However, another individual may have a karmic link with the same person that was bound with love & caring on both sides. In this instance, the relationship, on the surface, seems to be of love & compassion. "On the surface" refers to the fact that although the relationship was bound in the past with certain intentions, the end result could be very different!

At the time the actual coming together of scientific circumstantial evidences occurs, the new intentions or opinions which are formed determine the true quality of that relationship in the next life. A spiteful & caustic relationship between a brother & sister on the outside may appear ugly, however, on the inside, they may be both wishing that things were different and it should not be this way. Then, the end result of that relationship is actually positive. On the other hand, a loving & caring relationship between a husband & wife on the outside could appear beautiful, however, on the inside the couple could be binding revengeful intentions. The end result of that relationship actually is negative. Without being vigilant and "in the center", it is extremely difficult to determine the "true" nature of a relationship. Our goal is to bring the account balances to "zero". We must be especially wary where there is attachment, for that's where we tend to get caught! It is more difficult to bring the account balances to "zero" where there is attachment because it feels good! It makes good... and we like it! On the other hand, the karmic links that are bound out of detachment, with awareness, are quite deciduous. Those leaves fall of the tree without a trace and we do not even miss them!

Verse #5

"The fault lay with the sufferer is an undisputable natural law... Blame not the innocent instrument."

❧

Reflective Flashes—

This is yet another extremely bitter pill to swallow not only for ourselves but even for what we see of other's pain and suffering in the world. We witness world hunger, aids and all kinds of injustice and our hearts feel pangs of sadness. Why? Why does it have to be this way? Why the chaos? Why the useless waste of food when millions are starving? Why the lack of education in third world countries? There is a macro and a micro view for the fault lay with the sufferer. The macro one can be pacified as it does not directly affect us.

However, when we feel personal agony, pain and suffering, it is only with the power of pure knowledge and compassion of a Gyani that we can see it as our own fault. For many years my intellect convinced me that all the pain that I had suffered throughout my childhood was at least partially the fault of my parents for they had not protected me when I was young. My intellect would have wars with me. Even today, if I allow it to raise its ugly head... it will try. I have to gently cajole my intellect to peacefully sit aside for my parents and the perpetrator were only innocent instruments. It is apparent through the pure knowledge of the Science of Absolutism that the fault was my own, although it may have been bound out of ignorance. I suffered in ignorance as a five year old little girl... and later with relative knowledge as a young lady and finally the suffering was wiped-out with pure knowledge as an adult. The end result was very positive! Whatever crime it was from the past... it resulted in the infinite bliss of the Pure Soul. Learn to see the positive results of the pain that you are suffering. Turn those thorns into fragrant smelling petals by allowing the Pure Soul to illuminate the positive side of those negatives that are tormenting you. Remember, the pain in our lives is only a vitamin for the Pure Soul! The innocent instruments causing any pain are only delivering our personally endorsed bills! We knowingly or unknowingly asked for it!

Verse #6

"To be poignantly humble in the relative world is the golden key to attain eternal freedom; in return on the other side, the beauty & grace of the 'real' will automatically and naturally grant a pedestal at the highest level."

ॐ

Reflective Flashes—

Gases naturally rise as they have the least mass of all elements in the periodic table. They are responsible for all those beautiful skies we see that are filled with different shades of red, purple and orange. That beautiful eye candy is really the mixture of gases way up in the atmosphere creating a free-of-cost show for us as we gaze in admiration. What effort did those gases make? None. They were just in their natural state and got mixed around with other gases to create natural beauty.

Similarly, the Pure Soul is by its very nature lighter than the lightest split atom. The Pure Soul is absolutely humble. There is not a speck of relative contaminated ego in Pure Soul.

However, there is 'relative' ego in the 'relative' Self. The more humble we become in the relative, the closer we get to living as one with Pure Soul. There is no ego worth keeping in the 'relative' besides 'I do not want to cause any pain to any living being through this mind, body and speech.' That is the only ego worth keeping. Otherwise, all the other hats we wear operate on 'dramatic' ego. They do not need any further fuel. As a matter of fact, they actually operate better without 'our' interference.

If we decide that it is our place to be at the epitome of humility in the relative, like the gases, we will rise above everything... be able to know-and-see all that occurs and naturally, as a by-product paint a beautiful life of dignity, honor and grace for all to view without any effort at all!

Verse #7

"If a true torchbearer of self-knowledge (Gyani Purush) can be found, all will automatically be surrendered. Liberation or complete freedom will commence from the moment of complete and unequivocal surrender."

❧

Reflective Flashes—

How can we recognize a "true" torchbearer of self-knowledge (Gyani Purush)? This is the ultimate litmus test for our level of internal development. This is a path of the heart and Soul, not the intellect. We need intellect to understand to a certain level, however, there are those who do not even need that! They are drawn by the purity of their hearts to the 'Gyani Purush'. It is much easier for the 'Gyani' to write the eternal truth on such a clean slate than on that of a Ph. D. or Master's degree holder! The first and foremost criteria is that a true 'Gyani' has not an iota of expectation or desire from anything or any one. He is not even insistent that we sit with him. He is divinely humble to the point of being like a small child, completely unassuming and without any external ego. Ego is what makes people look ugly! The 'Gyani' is ever fresh and never looks like a wilted flower or a castor oil face! The speech of a 'Gyani' is completely from the center. No one will object to His words for they are completely non-harming in nature and go straight to the heart of the listener.
The recognition is key, thereafter follows the complete surrender. In order to get maximum value from the 'Gyani' the surrender must be unequivocal. The complete experience of true freedom is directly proportional to the level of complete surrender. He asks you to leave all your pain, suffering, worry and strife of life at His divine feet and bestows upon you the sparkling diamond of Pure Soul. What an exchange!
What do we have to lose? Nothing! He is taking it all upon His shoulders providing that we live within His five divine dictates which do not require us to 'do' anything. We just need to keep an awareness of these five divine dictates. What a deal! It is better than 'Wheel of Fortune' or 'Who Want's to be a Millionaire'!

Verse #8

"The past is just that : passed! The future is in the hands of an impartial cosmic computer powered by very minute karmic matter and manifested by the meeting of scientific circumstantial evidences. This energy is called 'vyavasthit' in the Science of Absolutism; Only the present moment is yours to experience & utilize to the fullest for the quest of pure infinite knowledge."

ॐ

Reflective Flashes—

We live our lives with the echoes of the past. They haunt us. We have labels which resound in our minds... some that are positive and some that torment our inner being. Some of us live in denial and the baggage inside has been stuffed so deep that it has given rise to physical ailments and mental illness. This is not a path of repression or sublimation; we need to deal with the baggage. The beauty is that we now have the tools to overcome all those skeletons hanging in the closet and get over the traumas of the past that force us to live the life of a bandit on the run! Running from what? Our own past!

Through the use of heartfelt prayer and penance for our past mistakes, the past will no longer haunt.

Once the 'Gyani' bestows the unequivocal pedestal of Pure Soul through His divine separation key, our future is in the hands of an impartial cosmic computer software that has already been programmed and has begun playing on automatic cue. It cannot be stopped and it cannot be altered. It has already been programmed to execute. Your own karma, intentions, sins and good deeds determined the creation of the software that is now running on auto.

So, fear not, all is within the divine power of nature's ultimate justice. Be prepared to face the fruit of your deeds whatever they may be!

Finally, the present is ours! We have now been given the royal throne of Pure Soul. What a priceless diamond! We may even fail to recognize the immense value of this diamond because of our shortsighted vision and imploring need for the pleasure of the five senses. Waste not a moment! Take charge of the File #1 and maintain your royal seat and enjoy boundless bliss!

Verse #9

"No one is your overhead or boss, you by your very nature are independent;
Your false beliefs & mistakes are your only overhead."

৵

Reflective Flashes —

What about all the noise going on in our heads and the people in our lives who make our heart have tremors? It does not feel like independence! Not until we are seated 'exactly' in the center will the experience of complete independence take place. That means 'we' are completely 'separate' from our File #1 (for me it is Shaila). When someone insults 'Shaila' or hurts her feelings, 'we' know-see-perceive what is occurring and perhaps even give 'Shaila' a little pat on the shoulder and say, 'It's okay... your accounts are being cleared. Don't worry 'we' are with you.' Furthermore, it is absolutely necessary to have complete reverence for and humility with every living being including ants and mosquitoes.

What are our biggest false beliefs and mistakes? The biggest false belief is that 'I am this person called _____.' Other wrong beliefs are 'I am this boy's mother. I am this man's daughter. I am this woman's daughter. I am a sister. He is my brother.' The list goes on and on. We cannot get rid of these false beliefs and mistakes on our own. Mistakes take the form of 'I did this'; 'Without me this family would be a wreck.'; 'What would they do without me?'; 'I work so hard.'; 'I suffered so much.'; 'They have wronged me.' These are all mistakes. From the moment 'we' take ownership, the plague of self-ignorance and suffering begins. It is important to note that a person who has not realized Pure Soul from the Gyani cannot say 'Not mine.' That person would go insane because they wouldn't know where to put the 'I' that they are renouncing. It's like giving up your seat in the 'relative' and not having a 'real' one to sit on! This concept is to be understood more than anything else.

When we let our attachments and detachments rattle our being,, we are making a mistake! We ha she experiences attachment and detachment. This is how we allow mistakes and we stepped into the foreign realm of 'relative' self. We must 'see' and 'know' Shaila when wrong beliefs to become our overhead. This mind, body and speech will one day become one with the mother earth. That is where it came from. That cannot be our permanent Self because it does not even belong to us! What outrageous wrong beliefs we have been raised with in this relative world! So, free yourself and fly high as an independent Pure Soul! Just see... your relative Self... in all the phases of life and throughout each and every day. It is a very beautiful, natural process if we allow it to be with the guiding light of pure knowledge and understanding.

Verse #10

"If you are simple & straightforward, the world will be so as well; If you are complex & difficult, the world will be so as well; The world is distinctly and exactly without fault or flaw, it is exact."

و‌ه‌

Reflective Flashes—

We hear the cliché, 'Simplify your life.' That is not what we are talking about here. It can help to simplify. However, what we are talking about is what is inside you. If your heart is clear and your intentions are clear... you are simple and straightforward. Transparency is key. What is on the outside should be on the inside and vice-versa! This is an anomaly in this day and age. It sounds so trivial and almost irrelevant to the attainment of Pure Soul, however, it is paramount. Without becoming transparent, it is impossible to attain liberation.

Our minds show us everything that is wrong... wrong with us... wrong with others... wrong in the world. Our minds are imperfect. Our minds cannot grasp the scope of the exactness of this world. Only the heart can truly absorb the truth of exactness and the 100% justice in each and every happening. When the robber goes free... that is exact. The robber is stealing as a result of that other person's sin and his own intention to steal. He may pay later or may not. It depends on his intentions. He may sincerely repent for what he is doing. Aladdin stole in order to keep from rotting away, out of necessity. Did he want to do it? No. His heart was pure and noble. His spirit was extremely generous.

What appears on the outside is not even a glimpse of the depth of this universe. If we quiet our minds and listen with our hearts, it is possible to experience the exactness of this universe. Furthermore, if we have the realization of Pure Soul, we will experience a crystal clear vision of the exact nature of this universal truth. If you have not found a 'Gyani' or Absolute Scientist, make it your life mission to find one who can give you your Pure Soul in the palm of your hand!

Verse #11

"Take not anything with undue force, for struggle and strife cause blood to drip; That which occurs naturally and effortlessly is most beneficial and least harmful."

⚬

Reflective Flashes—

Whatever happens without any conflict or trouble is most beneficial to you and those around you. It is not necessary to cause waves in order to obtain complete freedom. Have you every wanted something so bad that you did everything in your power to make it happen (or so you thought)? Whether you got it or not... was it worth it? The worst part is the scheming, plotting and negative intentions that may have been bound in that quest.

You may really have wanted to marry some person. And they were already with someone else. All the plotting and scheming to steal that person from another itself is so harmful! Let alone the revenge that is ignited in the other person who is losing the one they really wanted. Furthermore, if you are unsuccessful in your attempt, the feelings of revenge that you will bind towards the person you so wanted at one time! Not to mention, the person who you were looking to take them away from! It is an ugly circle!

Accept that which comes to you naturally. It is in your favor. It is of your right. It is suicidal to the quest for the Pure Soul to pine for something that truly does not belong to you whether it is a person or a material belonging. No matter what you do; that which does not belong to you will not stay with you!

Why live a life of a beggar? Be like a king or queen and accept that which comes to you naturally and live like royalty with nobility and integrity for yourself and others.

A dog attempts to suck the juice from a bone. The bone has none! It is free from any flesh or blood. How could it? Instead, the dog ends up sucking it's own blood as a result of the hardness of the bone believing it to be from the bone! How ludicrous is that? That is what it is like to want something or someone that does not belong to us! We are literally sucking our own blood (harming ourselves in countless ways) and believe that we are accomplishing something that gives us pleasure.

Verse #12

"Everyday living involves give & take, it goes on relentlessly; In the 'real' quest of pure eternal knowledge there is no give & take."

༄

Reflective Flashes—

What goes on in the world is 'relative', there is no 'real' in relative transitory circumstances. The sad thing is people are looking for 'real' in the relative. How can that be found? How can you find the permanent in the temporaries? People are ultimately searching for unconditional love and permanent joy. That cannot be found in the relative world. It can only be found at the feet of an Absolute Scientist or 'Gyani'.

In the language of the 'real' there is no debits and credits. Only 'pure' untainted eternal love, knowledge, vision and compassion are to be found in the realm of the Pure Soul and at the feet of a 'Gyani'.

An Absolute Scientist has no expectation for anything in return for the pure knowledge, vision and joy that are graced upon the fortunate receiver. For, the grace is only instrumental. He is in a complete spirit of 'instrumental' giving. The receiving is natural and directly proportionate to the level of development of the receiver. The receiver 'owes' nothing to the 'Gyani' for the 'Gyani' does not consider himself 'separate' from the receiver. The Absolute Scientist lives in a state of complete 'oneness' with every living being in the entire universe.

Therefore, in order to truly find oneself, one must first lose oneself in the relative sense. This means that we must become completely and divinely humble in the relative world to be firmly seated in the Pure Soul and experience the infinite knowledge, vision, energy and bliss that is integral to the Pure Soul's nature. In other words, we need to get over ourselves and our desires for fame, wealth and prestige!

Verse #13

"Restraining from interference will lead to a life without disturbance from anyone; Accept and enjoy that which flows to you naturally without struggle."

✣

Reflective Flashes—

Saving the world can only be done with ardent and heartfelt prayer. Furthermore, the 'saving' or any part of it is only 'instrumental' otherwise, there is no benefit. Some of us interfere in a quest for justice or what is right. Then we learn that even if we put our hand too close to the fire by accident, we get burned!

We want our children not to suffer the same trials and tribulations we have suffered. That is fair, however, we must not interfere with their development as human beings. We have all come with our own karma. If we attempt to repress or re-direct them without their own perceived free will; the ball will bounce back in our court. Meaning, we will endure the consequences whether they be good or bad. The goal is to bring the account balances to zero. It is our duty to show the pros and cons to our children and it is their decision which direction they will take. Fulfill your duties in your personal life with a professional attitude. Keep it clean and residue free. You will realize that the results will be quite crystal. Otherwise, do not be surprised if your role as a parent, spouse or child becomes a plague. Do not overstep your boundaries in the relative world. Live in normality and do not stick your nose where it does not belong! Have you ever been pleasantly surprised? There is no feeling that equals that wonderful joy that is felt in the relative life from a 'pleasant' surprise. If we maintain a policy of 'everything is ok' and 'we are fine' in all circumstances, most of life will become a pleasant surprise! In this day-and-age, there really is no such thing as 'real' pain besides of course a tragedy or physical pain. We have automatic cars. We can eat whatever we feel like! We have air conditioners and heaters. We have tools to make it easy to study, read, even exercise! This life is a gift. With the knowledge and awareness of the Pure Soul, this life is a miracle. Do not waste it. Get your accounts cleared while the going is good!

Verse #14

"Wear the divine shoes of knowledge on your tender feet, the thorns will not bother you. Live your life while wearing the golden spiritual shield of pure eternal knowledge."

❧

Reflective Flashes—

We have established we are here to clear the accounts. Our goal is to bring the account balances to zero. Our job is to live with that strong intention and goal. It is not in our hands to make it happen! The impartial cosmic computer software energy (vyavasthit shakti) is responsible to make that happen. As Pure Soul, we are knower-perceiver and in our own infinite bliss.

In this age of clash and conflict, it is easy to get pricked with thorns! There are plenty to be found everywhere we go. It is prudent, practical and moral to wear the divine shoes of knowledge at all times! Once we get burned from the heat of fire or bleed from the pricking of thorns, we will realize danger of stepping out of those divine shoes.

It is not worth searching for pleasure of the senses in this world that is burning out-of-control in the throws of greed, lust, hatred, and revenge. We want to make a difference in the world with our altruistic thinking. However, how can a single fireman put out a raging fire? The fireman will lose his own life in that quest. Instead, that fireman is wise to sit aside and take care of himself, his family and pray for the knowledge of the Pure Soul. This fire is such that cannot be seen with the human eyes, however, can burn you alive and exile your soul to a life in hell. Beware!

No man has the power to do anything in this world! People are weak. They are like animals in the jungle just striving to survive and maintain their own needs, pleasures and egos. It is a royal feat to live decently in an indecent world. The world will is such that will give awards to those who cause divorces, encourage drugs, prostitution and gambling; and encourage people to be immoral. Have you ever noticed this about this place we call 'our' world?

If you have pure knowledge from a 'Gyani', live with that protective shield and get freedom while you are able. If you do not, make it a life mission to find a 'Gyani' who can give you that pure knowledge.

Verse #15

"Relative life is a trap from which there is no relief; Stay firmly planted in the center in the seat of the Pure Soul."

❧

Reflective Flashes—

We know this... yet... we get lulled into it! We still search for that little bit of pleasure on earth in this relative life. It's that little doggy instinct that is so prevalent in today's world. How can we suck just a little more juice out of a doggy bone that truly has none? How sad!

When we realize that life is only a drama; seriously ONLY a drama and everything is temporary and fleeting except the Pure Soul; we will begin our true journey. There is infinite joy, peace, knowledge and vision in our 'real' home. Then, why do we stray? We stray because for infinite lives we have lived this way! We have searched high and low for permanent happiness and have not found it! How could we in a temporary life with temporary pleasures in a temporary ever-changing world? It was nowhere to be found!

The minute we 'identify' with our circumstances, the pain starts. The intellect suddenly gets a license to show us the pros and cons (mostly cons). The mind starts pushing our buttons and our relative ego will start doing summersaults! Then, we start trouble with our family and friends without any good reason except that we have left our royal seat of the Pure Soul. Then, we must repent and dutifully make prayers to clean up the mess we have made!

No matter how tempting it is, do not get lulled by the relative pleasures and the illusion of the relative world. It will come back to bite in a big way! You will have lost that much of your progress in the realm of infinite permanent bliss. Furthermore, whenever you 'fail' (in real knowledge) in a particular circumstance, you must go through that again until you pass! It is like an examination. Be vigilant and vow to get through every exam the first time with a passing grade! In Dada's exams, you only need 60% for a passing grade! There are bigger and better things ahead! Do not get stuck in the relative.

Verse #16

"While in the pure spirit of 'I am Pure Soul', peel away the layers of relative life; Wherever there is a lacking, fill it appropriately bringing balance to the scales of life."

☙

Reflective Flashes–

One of the most difficult aspects of parenting is discipline and tough love. If we TRULY care for our children, we allow them to grow and become independent, responsible individuals. We must allow them to fall at times and learn the difficult lessons of life. This is the process of allowing an individual to mature from a child, young adult to adult.

Similarly, while being seated in the golden throne of 'Pure Soul' we must allow our relative self to pass through the circumstances and peel away the layers of relative life. The ultimate goal is when the relative self becomes 'one' with the Pure Soul (us). The 'Gyani Purush' (Dada Bhagavan) was short 4 degrees from 360 degrees meaning his 'relative' self 'Ambalal Muljibhai Patel' was imperfect by 4 degrees due to his desire to be an instrument for establishing 'real' well-being in the world. For infinite lives He had searched for a way to enable people to attain liberation while living the worldly life. This is His gift to us at no cost to us! The more degrees we accumulate, the more oneness with 'Pure Soul' the relative self has attained and greater freedom will be experienced!

It is important for us to be vigilant and not allow the mind to take us for a ride! It is important to be vigilant in the same manner with the intellect. It is not the fault of the mind or the intellect, that is their nature! They look for trouble... that is the very nature of mind and intellect to show the debits and credits. We must bring balance by continually throughout the day engaging in 'real' effort to stay seated in the center at the Pure Soul and not allow the relative self get the upper hand! How? Through the five divine dictates and other devotional tools which have been given to us! Did you know singing one paad of Kavi Raj is equivalent to a samayik? When the system breaks down, bring on the tool box!

Verse #17

"Relative life is unsettling from the core, it's a game of give and take; No one 'real'-ly belongs to anyone here."

ﻼ

Reflective Flashes—

Common sense is key. In order to get through this game we call life... we must cultivate our common sense. This can be accomplished by keeping it simple, curbing our intellect from working overtime and keeping our goal for clearing the accounts before us at all times.

Even those we love dearly in our hearts are only accounts to be settled in the relative. We cannot make the mistake of believing even those to be 'real'. The only 'real' is Pure Soul and our experience of Pure Soul. As we learn to see Pure Soul even in our worst enemy, we become acutely and keenly aware of the temporary 'relative' relationships and how they function.

In order to be 'free' from the negative effects of the game of give and take in the relative, it is crucial to hang our egos in the closet (with regards to the world) and be simple & straightforward in all our dealings with others. We must engage in a little 'self-talk' to keep the relative self in line. No, we are not out to steal from anyone in anyway. We are not out to prove ourselves superior to anyone. We are not even out there to better the world per se. Our only goal is to clear the accounts and bring the balances to zero with each and every living being that is even remotely associated with us. This is NOT something negative. It is actually a beautiful thing! When we free ourselves... we are also freeing others! They do not even know what is taking place but they, too, feel that little glimmer of freedom! Your association suddenly becomes a pure, unconditional one rather than one of worldly hum-drum 'give-and-take'.

The part about 'no one really belongs to anyone' here is not designed to be used in a negative fashion. This is a fact. It is much more beneficial to take that nugget and use it when someone we have attachment for may become an instrument of pain to us. Use the knowledge in a positive fashion for that is the purpose for it.

Verse #18

"There is none in this world that can hinder or control circumstances; 'The flow of events' is out of the realm of one's control."

⚜

Reflective Flashes —

We all want to believe we are in control of our lives and the events that take place in them. It is true! Especially in this day-and-age of clash and quarrel! We will hear things like, 'I did it because I wanted to!'; 'You are not my boss.'; 'You can't control my life.'; 'I can do whatever I want!'; 'I don't care. I will do whatever I feel like.' These are the kinds of statements and exclamations people make. They want to believe that nobody and nothing controls them! The sad thing is they do not even know who they are! No wonder there is kaos!

The world operates on the intentions and desires of people. The impartial cosmic computer software that is currently executing on auto was designed with the intentions and desires of people. Those with large credit balances in their cosmic bank account easily and efficiently obtain their desires in the relative world. Those with low credit balances in their cosmic bank account are more challenged in achieving their objectives. The more struggle and strife there is in life, the less the credit balance in the cosmic bank account. The smartest one is not necessarily the wealthiest! Have you ever noticed this? The one with the most credit balance in the cosmic bank account is the wealthiest (monetarily). Now, we all have different definitions of wealth so it must be specified what kind of wealth we are referring to! So, events flow based on people's intentions, desires and credit/debit balances.

Unfortunately, the results we see today are based on seeds of intentions and desires which were planted in the past life or lives. When we get the results, we react and sometimes form different opinions or desires. Our goal is to end the cycle of forming opinions or desires that perpetuate the cycle of birth and death. Our only intention is to 'clear the accounts'! So, do not get all worked-up over circumstances and torture yourself and others with a façade of control. Be simple and straightforward, see and know the circumstances for what they are: a film. Stay seated in your golden throne of Pure Soul. Fear not! For nothing outside the realm of the laws of nature and the impartial cosmic computer can occur.

Verse #19

"Deflect all conflict from a distance; remove yourself with complete understanding from any conflict; If you clash, you lose the essence of the experience of the 'Pure Soul'."

ᴄᴀ

Reflective Flashes—

Once we have decided we would like to attain liberation, it is crucial to be aware of all the pitfalls. One of the biggest ones is knowingly engaging in conflict with any living being. Our understanding and eventually exact experience of the impartial cosmic computer which executes software based on people's intentions, desires and credit/debit balances will automatically enable us to step aside in the line of fire without any conflict. This is so much easier said than done! Like most things that are great and elevating... it takes keen awareness and understanding. There is subtle conflict arising from sensitivity with loved ones. This conflict is so subtle and minute that it is usually not visible to the human eye, however, has the power to give heart attacks. We must learn to put our 'sensitivity' aside and view the world from a 'pure' perspective. The 'pure' perspective of knowledge from a 'Gyani' enables us to deem even our closest files (loved ones) as innocent. Our intellect will show us all the reasons why we should feel bad, be hurt, end a relationship or just plain throw a tantrum. It is up to us to rise above that. We are all in survival mode at the end of the day. We each are responsible for our own pain and suffering whether it is mental, physical, and emotional or a combination thereof. If we take a stand and take 100% accountability for our own results, and ourselves we will be more successful in avoiding and deflecting conflict.

Make it a mission to avoid all conflict each and every morning when you rise. No matter what happens, we want to avoid clashing and conflicting with those closest to us. This applies to those that are closest to us where our emotional investment is very high. It is not meant for distant files... everyday acquaintances. Those are much easier to deal with anyways. There is less emotional investment with business contacts, neighbors, friends, community members and others.

Verse #20

*"The karmic relations of the past, fulfill your obligation to them with
a steady and firm intention to clear the account and bring the account
balance to a big beautiful zero."*

❧

Reflective Flashes—

In the language of pure knowledge there is no rhyme or reason except
clearing the accounts. It is all very natural and effortless. The ways of
the relative world will instigate our minds to think diametrically opposite
to this concept. The ways of today's world in particular are specifically
geared towards, 'What's in it for me right now or in this lifetime?' Our
conditioning gears us towards thinking ONLY in terms of our own comfort
and that of our own loved ones. This is not the way to liberation.

Yes, we must fulfill our worldly obligations to our family and in a very
sincere manner. However, the mentality is what needs to change! We are
not taking anything with us when we go back to mother earth. All we take
is whatever karmic baggage we have left at that point. Let's keep that to a
minimum so our last few lives will be light, beautiful and an example for the
world.

There are certain people in our lives that it seems no matter what we do or
say, it is wrong! Those are our 'sticky' files. In our past, we had wronged or
badgered them in a big way. It does not have to be the same soul, although,
it can be if it is that 'sticky', however, the pain or injustice we inflicted
is what we are paying for. That person is just an instrument and totally
innocent. Therefore, it behooves us to engage in sincere and heartfelt
prayer to the Pure Soul of that being in order to free both from this
uncomfortable bondage. What a great opportunity to be an instrument
in the quest for liberation! The beauty of it is that the other person is
elevated and freed as well due to our heartfelt and pure prayer without any
effort on their part.

In the language of the world, 'zero' is not such a beautiful thing! It is ironic
that an Indian man actually brought the concept of zero to the world and
thus numbers! Zero is where we would like to take the relative account so
we can be infinite (alpha) in the 'real'!

Verse #21

"Natural human tendencies are as diverse as the different kinds of flowers available through mother nature, even the colors and designs are myriad; Exist and stay separate as 'knower-perceiver-seer' only."

ৎ৯

Reflective Flashes—

There is so much to know and see! The paradox is that you are not a true knower-perceiver unless you are seeing and knowing your relative self! Did you know everything in the entire universe is within you? According to pure knowledge of the Pure Soul, there is nothing else to be truly known and seen except oneself (one's file #1). When we remain as knower-perceiver of our relative self, the entire universe and all it's objects begin to sparkle. The reason for this is we are truly knower-perceivers at that point. This is an extremely subtle concept, but once it is grasped... the journey becomes quite incredible!

In essence, only when we are seated completely at the center of the sphere (in the divine throne of Pure Soul) are we truly seeing-and-knowing everything "as it is" in the universe including our relative self. What a beautiful concept!

It is helpful even without divine knowledge from an Absolute Scientist to see and know all the different personality types and understand that they are innocent. They are acting out of the forces of nature, of their own design based on their intentions, desires, good deeds and bad deeds from the past. Nature has such a tremendous task of designing all these incredibly unique and diverse personalities and looks! It is ironic how the human ego works. We understand that nature creates flowers a certain way. We even went as far as grafting to create hybrids through our knowledge of genetics. Humans are so egotistical that they have to put their hands in everything and feel that they have power over it by exploiting it! What we do not realize is that we are a product of the same force! Ultimately no body has the power that the laws of nature have in this universe. What is that force behind the laws of nature? It is once again the impartial cosmic computer and its software (vyavasthit shakti) that are at work.

Verse #22

"You are Pure Soul, everything else is circumstantial, seal and cement that understanding. Circumstances are all to be seen & known exactly as they truly are without any illusion."

ॐ

Reflective Flashes—

When we are sleeping, we understand that our dreams are not real. We are aware that they are a result of our subconscious mind's activity and processing methodology. Our dreams really show us what we have seen before or will see in the future. Of course, it is not literally what we have seen or will see, but in pieces and segments sometimes all jumbled up! Well, when we sleep, we are aware of our status as knower-perceiver from an intellectual standpoint even without knowledge of Pure Soul. The same applies when we are awake except in this 'dream' we are part of the drama that is taking place. It really is NO different! If this can be fully understood, it will serve to seal and cement the understanding of our permanent and undisputable identity as Pure Soul amidst all these temporaries.

We all want other people to like us. This is a self-esteem issue. This also is a result of self-ignorance. We do not know who we really are and believe the relative self to be our being. Of course, we want people to like us. We search for love on every corner if we did not get it where we expected it the most! On the other hand, if everyone does like us it is usually because we say 'yes' to everyone all the time and are considered one of those 'pushover' people. Either way, this is a result, it is a product of past karma. With pure knowledge, however, we learn to say 'yes' not because we want people to like us but because we want to be free! This is an example of action by true understanding rather than through blind ignorance. Once we have realized our Pure Soul from the 'Gyani', our only goal is to clear the accounts. It really does not matter if people think we are pushovers or not. What counts is that the account gets cleared! Wow... how freeing is that?

There are six elements in the world including fire, water, earth, air, the energy that makes things move (gati-sahayik) and the energy that makes things stop (gati-sthitayik). In order to be true Absolute Scientist protégés we must learn to see the world in terms of elements and Pure Soul. After all, that is all there really is!

Verse #23

" 'I and my' 'My and I', this emphasis perpetuates the relative life;
Surrender 'I and my' at the feet of the 'Absolute Scientist'."

ॐ

Reflective Flashes —

Our minds go on relentlessly generating thoughts without any consent from us. This is because the relative self is bombarded with relative things. It is dependent on and connected to the relative world. It is a somewhat symbiotic relationship with the relative world and the relative self. When people do not process their anger, pride, attachment, detachment in an appropriate manner, the health problems start popping up and even mental illnesses can manifest. It is all extremely scientific and exact. The mind, body and spirit are directly related to each other and to the world.

It can be extremely difficult to manage our enemies such as anger, pride, attachment, detachment and greed in a healthy manner when we are actually unaware that they are an enemy to begin with! With the power of this pure knowledge, a separation occurs that allows one to see one's own faults. This is unheard of! Nobody can, let alone wants to see their own faults in this ego-driven world! This is where humility once again plays a crucial role. We must take all of our 'I and my' affiliations and surrender them unconditionally and completely at the feet of the Absolute Scientist. That is the only way we will truly experience pure independence. Through unequivocal and unconditional surrender we can experience independence from even the relative self that faces the world everyday. Make your relative self your best friend by being a true friend. A true friend would never let a friend head in the wrong direction or allow a friend to live in illusion. A true friend will show a friend a fault when necessary. There is a transparency that is rare and profound with the power of this pure knowledge.

Once the complete surrender occurs, life will feel like a light-hearted sitcom (extremely dramatic) and nothing really will touch deep down causing scarring like it has for infinite lives. The mind will still continue it's though processes, however, as we develop practice in staying seated in the Pure Soul at all times, it will lose it's power to lead us down the wrong path.

Verse #24

"The viewpoint determines the perception of the universe; the universe is completely innocent (without fault); Fix your flawed vision to commence your journey to the eternal."

ॐ

Reflective Flashes—

Our attachment and detachment ingrained from the past are huge obstacles to viewing the world with a clear and unbiased standpoint. Also, the pain and suffering we have suffered as a result of others also is a huge roadblock! The scars in our heart make us emotional and skew our vision if we are not vigilant and do not remain 'observer' of those scars and the latent ashes that are still red from heat. Yes, most of us have these scars whether we like to admit it or not. The scars heal but are still visible! They never really go away... there is always a reminder right before our eyes. It is sad but true. We must learn to see them as a blessing to remind us of the temporary nature of the relative life. They also serve to remind us not to become engrossed in attachment and detachment. Those scars originated because of attachment and detachment. We definitely do not want to go there again!

It is crucial to understand from the core of our being to understand the COMPLETE innocence of the world. The fault is our own. After all, our life is our own projection on the belief that we were someone we really were not in our past life. We created this with our own opinions, intentions, good deeds and bad deeds. Now, when that dear mail person delivers the goods we ordered... we cannot blame them! It really is that simple. The world is 100% innocent; the fault lay within. Why suffer two losses? We have to suffer the consequences of our own mistakes and blunders but why suffer twice? Let's not fall into the same trap again! We know better now. The true journey begins when all the fingers are pointing inward and the world is truly viewed as 100% innocent. It does not mean we walk around like jellies and agree with everything everyone says and do everything everyone asks of us. It means, internally, we do not hold grudges; we do not harbor feelings of revenge; and finally regardless of what occurs on the outside, we see the Pure Soul of each and every living being. It is a beautiful journey to be able to see the Pure Soul of someone who is considered an enemy or competitor in the relative world. It becomes a true drama rather than a bitter and cheated life. Cheating who? Our own Pure Soul.

Verse #25

"The entire world is completely without fault, only you yourself are at fault; With this simple truth, bliss eternal prevails."

ॐ

Reflective Flashes—

This quote brings to memory an incident that occurred when I was sixteen with my father. One of my goals as a young adult was to be doctor. So, being relatively pro-active, I decided to volunteer at the local hospital in Anaheim, CA. I had been volunteering for 3 years doing candy striping and in the gift shop and I had a little conflict. I was doing a shift in the gift shop and a friend came to visit me there. A few of the nurses saw them visiting with me and reported me to my supervisor. The volunteer organization is mainly made-up of elderly retired women. I was the only young person there. She called me into her office and chastised me. I was quite taken back as I had been volunteering for years and never even got paid! I went home and told my dad about what happened. To my horror, he said to me, 'I want you to go to that dear lady and thank her for showing you your own mistake and ask for forgiveness.' I did not appreciate my dad too much at that time, however, he did teach me a valuable lesson. I did end up apologizing and things were fine.

There are several lessons that I learned from this. First of all, no matter what you do in life. Do it sincerely! Whether you are paid or not, you are responsible and accountable in all aspects. Furthermore, be careful of your friends. Sometimes those that you consider your 'friends' could be the instruments to your doom. Be aware of who you choose to walk with! Finally, this little teaching opportunity for my dad taught me to take responsibility for all the things that happen to me in my lifetime. How many of you have little stories like that? Yeah... we try to forget but they stick with us!

It all boils down to how much progress you want to make as a human being. God is really 100% human. What is the definition of human? It is being aware of and concerned about how your own behavior through mind, speech and action will impact others. If you are 100% human, then you truly are one with Pure Soul otherwise known as God. Let' at least take the first step towards this goal by keeping our fingers pointed inward.

Verse #26

"The entire universe is perfectly synchronized, the knower/perceiver remains unaffected; Know & see, do not open the flood gates and allow anything to flow in and touch 'you' at the inner core."

৵

Reflective Flashes—

This does not mean we are inhibit to relative self. No... no not all! The relative self can shed tears, can should be allowed to feel everything. This is not a path of repression or sublimation. Life is to be lived to the fullest. If you like to play tennis, golf, white water raft, sky dive or any other activity, the relative self has the liberty. The only thing to be fearful of is sex, sex-related attractions outside of marriage, alcohol and drugs. This is a danger zone. Having attachment to things or activities is tolerable because things will not come looking for us or harbor feelings of revenge or hatred. This is extremely important and cannot be emphasized enough! If there was a path of destruction and complete spiritual suicide... it is engaging in unacceptable sexual activity of any sort. It is not okay to remain a knower-perceiver when it comes to this. With this particular aspect of life, we must be vigilant and even give rise to ego if necessary to keep us clean. It is okay only to engage in sexual activity with our spouse. If we are single, it is not okay at all with anyone. The reason for this is that humans hold grudges and harbor feelings of hatred and revenge especially when it comes to something as intrusive and personal as sex. Even if the person claims it is no big deal, it really is. That is human nature to the core. There is no such thing as casual sex because it is the primary cause of bondage with another living being.

So, the entire universe is perfectly synchronized. It is a direct reflection of our own projections. We must be careful and vigilant when it comes to attraction with regards to other people. Our relative self becomes totally engrossed at that time and forgets the whole world including the Pure Soul. At that time, it is crucial to oppose and not encourage the relative self. Engage in self-talk in the mirror. Let the relative self that you are not with them. This verse is quite self-explanatory so it was important to include the exclusions: sex, drugs and alcohol.

Otherwise, watch the relative self in all aspects and phases. It is okay to even watch what occurs in the world. Remain cool and neutral. Do not form opinions of any sort. It is not worth it! The only intention worth keeping is to clear the accounts! Just 'see & know' your relative self in all aspects and phases of life from childhood, youth, adult to senior. Allow your relative self to live-out fully all the phases of life in a natural and customary manner. Do not allow any activities which you would not do in front of your parents, children or grandchildren. This is the thermometer.

Verse #27

"Do not hold onto anything, stay unassuming to live a path of simplicity &
straightforwardness. The necessities will come to you naturally from your
credit balance in the impartial universal cosmic computer bank account."

༈

Reflective Flashes —

There are certain events and incidents that leave a lasting impression.
They go to the very core of your heart and leave their scars. It is extremely
difficult to heal, let alone forget these happenings. Sometimes it can even
be a dream that haunts our being. We cannot seem to shake it. It is like a
plague and makes us abrupt, discontent and cynical. We must let go for
our own well being! The path to dysfunction will start sprouting all sorts
of tentacles in every direction if we allow them the liberty. Stop the cycle
once and for all! We all have these hang-ups and we know what they are.
Let them go!!! The reason we cannot let go is that our minds, hearts and/or
egos were fractured by these events or incidents. It takes the grace and
compassion of the Absolute Scientist and the God (Pure Soul) within to
heal these awful cracks and faults.
Once you decide to let it all go engage in devotional practices of the Pure
Soul to help heal those wounds. It does work.
We all worry about our future. We would not have retirement accounts,
educational funds for our children or life insurance if we did not think
about the future and the 'what ifs' of life. These are relative practices that
most prudent people engage in. There is nothing to be analyzed here.
However, it is important to keep in mind the workings of the impartial
universal cosmic computer. Nothing happens outside of its intricate
workings. In other words, it is not worth getting an ulcer worrying over
anything. It is all within the workings of nature.
No one belongs to anyone here! Ultimately we are all on our own. What
we gave is what we get in this lifetime. It is a simple hard candy to swallow!
Have you ever tried to swallow hard candy? It hurts. What is important to
remember is no matter how hard it is, it is still sweet. You are able to taste
the sweetness if you slowly let it dissolve in your mouth. This means we
must live with awareness and alertness of the pure eternal knowledge and
it's principles.

Verse #28

"Where there is ego, there is no soul, the egotistical can never attain freedom; therefore, surrender your ego at the feet of the Absolute Scientist or 'Gyani Purush'."

ॐ

Reflective Flashes—

No matter how we slice it, life is a paradox. You cannot be without an ego, yet with falsely placed ego, you are miserable! 99.99% of the people in the world, if not more, have their egos in a falsely projected place. They cannot have it anywhere else because they do not know, 'Who Am I'. When this is known, then the 'real' ego is at the right place and the dramatic ego remains. It sounds so simple yet is so profound and rare it eludes us for infinite lifetimes! Without the enlightened Absolute Scientist it is not possible to realize one's true identity.

It is very beneficial to have humility and cultivate humility in the relative world by having reverence for every living being. Also, eating healthy vegetarian food will enable humility to manifest. In order to be humble, one must be light. It is without saying that eating vegetarian food will lighten the relative self in a hurry! After all, we have all heard: 'you are what you eat'. If you eat animal flesh you will become animal-like in your instincts. If you eat fruits, vegetables and grains, there is less pain inflicted on those living beings as they have less senses. You can hear the cries of a chicken or pig being slaughtered. You cannot hear the cries of a potato, onion or wheat as it is being plucked. Remember—You must make the relative self your best friend on the path to liberation. This means ultimately the relative self will become one with the Pure Soul. That is the goal. The beneficial habits must be cultivated and the harmful one's in the quest for Pure Soul must slowly be put down to rest forever. With the power of this knowledge, this is possible with understanding and the grace & compassion of the Absolute Scientist.

If you truly want to be free and attain oneness with the Pure Soul, seek to be the lightest and humblest in the relative. All will free you if you satisfy their egos. After all, it is temporary and relative! Let it go! It means little compared to the beauty, grace, and eternal bliss of the Pure Soul that is met at the other side! Rock on to the real side!

Verse #29

"Equanimity & control with regards to anger, pride, attachment and greed is true equanimity; physical & mental discipline are called worldly renunciation or penance. Permanent bliss is not attained through worldly renunciation."

ॐ

Reflective Flashes —

Discipline is a quality that will ensure a person will encounter fewer obstacles and will have the strength to overcome the obstacles that are met. Discipline is a great quality, however, will not lead to permanent bliss. In order to attain permanent bliss there has to be a renouncing of anger, pride, attachment and greed. This is true renunciation! How many of us would get angry if a homeless person littered or left their body waste on our property? At that moment, would we remember the Pure Soul of that person or be outraged? The outrage probably comes first and then the slow realization of the Pure Soul within that living being. Better late than never! We are quite spoiled in this day and age. Our patience is thin. Our demands are great. We want things yesterday and want them our way. This is NOT the path to liberation. The path to liberation is one of simplicity and humility. Do not fool yourself into believing you are on the path without the certification of the 'Absolute Scientist'. Another decent thermometer is your loved ones. If they give you their stamp of approval in this day-and-age of clash, conflict and revenge, you might just be on your way! Are you unsatisfied with life? Do you still crave respect, fame, material wealth? Yes, those desires and wishes are those of the relative self. However, we cannot give our stamp of approval to those! Our only aim should be to clear the accounts. It all comes down to truly remaining in the royal throne of Pure Soul and 'knowing-seeing' the myriad of emotions, dreams, wants and antics of the relative self.

Furthermore, we are not to 'renounce' anything... except of course our disclaimers: unmarried sex, infidelity, drugs and alcohol. Allow the relative self to live like a big cat... wild and free! The relative self needs to be totally uninhibited and free to express life except for our exclusions (that lead to personal and spiritual suicide).

Verse #30

" 'Nothing belongs to me' or 'the entire universe belongs to me'; with one of these convictions... live your life."

৯৯

Reflective Flashes—

If we think about it the result of both convictions is the same. If nothing belongs to us then we are 'separate' as knower-perceiver and if everything belongs to us then there is no cause for any clash or conflict with anyone as we become one with the Pure Soul of each and every living being. So, again, we become the knower-perceiver of all the happenings. Both of the convictions lead us to the center of the sphere! The key is to become completely neutral, even with regards to your relative self.

Sincerity plays a tremendous role in the adoption of either of these convictions. There is a profound impact on the lives of the people around one who lives with either one of these convictions. The presence alone of such a person brings peace, joy and vision to any environment. The key is the absence of any excess ego and the realization of the Pure Soul. That individual actually lives as a Pure Soul and allows the relative self to dramatically fulfill the worldly 'dramatic' role. It is like a slow and potent gas that permeates the environment and will leave its effect for quite some time even after that individual has physically departed! What an incredible power! Without any magic or anything to be able to impact the lives of others in such a positive manner is a gift only the 'Absolute Scientist' can bestow.

The 'Akram Path' (Stepless Path) is so unique and brilliant that it has not manifested on this earth in over a million years! Freedom without renunciation of any of the regular worldly activities! Wow. It leaves you speechless!

So, live with the awareness of all or nothing and stick with that conviction. The result will still be divine either way. Either conviction will humble in the relative and elevate to the highest level in the real. A good thermometer is how many times in a day we actually see Pure Soul in the living beings we encounter and think of vs. how many times we fail to do this. Why miss such a brilliant opportunity? There is too much to lose and so much to be gained!

Verse #31

"You've arrived here with a pre-recorded movie blueprint, at the appropriate times, the different episodes of the film unravel. There is no real effort in effect or end product (projection of the film)."

❧

Reflective Flashes —

The impartial cosmic computer has software in the form of extremely minute atoms, which at the appropriate times will cause events to occur. The minute atoms when prompted come down at the appropriate time, space and material circumstances to bring about the relative dramas that we witness everyday. This applies at home, at school, at work, at play... everywhere! This impartial cosmic computer controls even things we do not like to mention. As intricate, if not more, is the inner working of this impartial cosmic computer than of the human body. The human body is amazing. It heals, it pumps blood, and it digests food, forms the waste products, and actually causes excretion. What energy makes that happen? It is the same energy!

When things happen, we often take them personally! The biggest ego in the world is to think that the world or even just our loved ones could not go on without us! The world has always gone on and always will! Our biggest contribution is our intentions! We admire people that accomplish great things in their lives. It is a result of their past karma and good deeds. Who knows what kind of karma they are binding for their next life. Therefore, the greatest gift of all to the world is to live in one's real home and golden throne of Pure Soul. To do nothing is the biggest feat to accomplish! Not in a literal sense but to have that awareness and perception at all times is a grand feat. The world is going on as we are... but to have the perception and awareness that 'I am not the doer' of any of this at all times is real vision. Of course, one must have realized 'Who Am I' before this can be accomplished or the poor soul will go bonkers.

So, those with pure knowledge sit back in your golden throne of Pure Soul and watch the film unravel. See your relative self play it's part and know-see the happenings as they occur for what they truly are: temporary circumstances. For those without pure knowledge, pray to meet an 'Absolute Scientist' who can free you from the cycle of birth-and-death once and for all.

Verse #32

"You are a guest of nature; live with that conviction. The essentials will automatically and effortlessly flow to you."

❦

Reflective Flashes—

Our time here is so temporary and fleeting and we get so bogged-down with the petty things we forget how precious and timeless that bitty time is! Make it a timeless life by living a divinely inspired life. Have reverence for the temple (your mind, body, spirit and speech) nature has provided you with. Have reverence for others.

Our petty mean minds will show us the faults of others at every step. 'That person never does anything for us! They always use us. Nobody ever does anything nice for us and we are always doing things for others.' This is the negative intellect taking over our minds! It really only harms us! We cannot allow the mind to control us. We must rise above and take subtle but firm control of the mind.

How do we behave if we are a guest at someone's home? We are courteous, kind, humble and respectful. We make sure we do not overstep our boundaries. This is a great measuring stick for how to live our lives in the relative world. Not just when we are guests for others but with everyone at all times. Think about how great our relationship with our spouse would be if we held that standard. What about with our parents? Our siblings? Our children? It would become quite a blissful life for all if we could learn to live like a guest of nature and the people who inhabit this world we live in. Suddenly things will appear so different. People will start treating each other differently. Shock yourself and shock others by holding to that reverent standard that we all know is deep within us of how to live as a guest of nature. The significance of little things we took for granted will suddenly be much clearer and profound. Looking into our children's eyes we will realize they too are guests of nature. There is no reason for clash or conflict. We are all here as guests of nature. Suddenly, everything in life will not be such a huge struggle. It does not have to be that way. Let go of all those preconceived notions of how life "should be" and just live a clash free and reverent life.

Verse #33

"In the relative world, there is 'good-bad'; the 'real' non-material world takes a different position. Attachment and detachment are the root cause of any bondage."

⚬

Reflective Flashes—

According to the language of the quest for the real, attachment and detachment are the real culprits to bondage. Without attachment and detachment, there is no bondage. If we really think about this, it really is very exact. Without any attachment and detachment, we would not bind any karma at all. Our lives would be very smooth and conflict-free. There would be no reason to fight with anyone. Our battles are always based on attachment and detachment. We either like someone's behavior or we don't. We believe something is right or wrong. We want to live a certain way or not. We like a certain standard of living. We like certain groups of people and do not like others. In the relative world, this is very normal, however, it is the root cause of bondage. Attachment and detachment cause us to form new opinions. If we are in the center, at the core with Pure Soul, our attachment and detachment start to peel away like the layers off an onion.

We are conditioned by our parents from a very young age to believe certain things are 'good' and certain things are 'bad'. We even pick up on their prejudices against different kinds of people and certain types of behavior. We subconsciously adopt these in our minds without even knowing it. Then, unless we're vigilant and alert, we pass on these neuroses to our children. It is a cycle. We must break the cycle. This is the new age of science and innovation. Leave the old behind and spring forward with a clean slate. The power of this pure knowledge can enable us to do this. It is easier to allow gravity to pull us down and slouch. However, it takes effort to maintain a good posture. Similarly, we must maintain a positive and high-reaching posture to enable our future generation to accomplish much in this needy world. We must lead by example.

Let's be BOLD and put-aside all our attachment and detachment and live a life of 'pure' reverence, stability and strength in the infinite power of the Pure Soul.

Verse #34

"The input of karmic intentions is within our realm of power, the output from the master cosmic computer of the universe is outside the sphere of our own power. What we sow now is what will be reaped."

❧

Reflective Flashes—

Once you have turned in your exam, there is nothing you can do to change the results. If you were sick or tired, it does not matter. The result will be the same. If you had a quarrel with your family before the test it does not matter, the result will still be the same. No matter what the excuse, once you have turned in your exam paper to the proctor, the results are final. You can take the exam again perhaps, however, you cannot change the outcome of the first round.

This same concept is also true in the law of karma. Whatever you have fed into the master computer will result in output that matches that exact flavor and spice. If you accidentally put salt in milk, is it possible to change that? No. If you accidentally squeeze lemon into yogurt, can that be reversed? No. We must bear the fruits of the seeds that we had sown in the past. Hopefully we planted some sweet seeds in with the bitter. Actually, on the path to liberation the bitter seeds are vitamins for the quest of the Pure Soul. They give rise to that thirst for an answer to the question, 'Who Am I?' Consider the bitter results as blessings in disguise.

Television can be a source of tremendous poison for the mind. The images that are viewed cause subtle desires, which can be a tremendous obstacle on the path to liberation. It is wise to be vigilant and alert when viewing any program on television. Furthermore, television stations actually run subliminal images in the background to get the viewer on a subconscious level. Bottom line, television can give rise to increased sexuality, desires to consume excessive food and other unhealthy habits. What about the effect that television has on 3rd world countries? People without shoes, education and proper nutrition view shows like *90210* and *Friends*. What kind of intentions and desires do you think they are binding? Beware of TV! Be aware of what you feed your inner computer. Remember the goal is to clear the accounts.

Verse #35

"Those who have understood have settled with a peaceful stance, those who have not understood continue to split hairs in dissent; Immerse & dissolve yourself in the bliss & beauty of the 'Pure Soul'."

৵৹

Reflective Flashes—

There are certain things in life we must accept. These are things we come to realize and that most people around us come to realize. They are not necessarily pretty things. Some things are better left unsaid and rather just understood. There is much ugliness in the world. There is child abuse, spousal abuse, violence, crime and just plain mean politics. We all deal with these either from a distance or with a more microscopic view everyday. It is not smart trying to save a world that is already raging in an inferno. We would get burnt to a crisp in that process! In other words, the only person worth changing is you. Do not set out to right the wrongs. That is not our duty. Our duty is to know the Pure Soul and know the relatives for what they are. Yes, if an opportunity in the relative arises where you can be an instrument for positive change... that is a beautiful thing! Go for it! If not, do not waste your time. Also, be careful that the opportunity does not give rise to ego! Then, it will actually be a disservice rather than a service. We are not to be frigid icicles in the relative world. When something touches our heart or makes it hurt, the greatest gift we can give is a heartfelt prayer. That is a contribution that can go a long way! The power of prayer cannot be stressed enough.

Stay seated on the golden throne of Pure Soul. That light, that power alone will transform your environment without any visible effort on your own part. This is a path of transformation without any doer ship. Just by seeing Pure Soul in each and every living being, divine transformations are in the working. This knowledge is so simple, yet we live in a such a complex world! That is the paradox of the situation. Use the power that we truly do possess and you will be witness to incredible transformations, first in yourself; then, in the world around you.

Verse #36

"Bliss boundless lay within, when that realization occurs; the quest for pleasure in the relative forever comes to a full stop."

༄

Reflective Flashes—

People constantly have to define and redefine who they are in order to stay current! The world is moving so quickly that it is difficult to keep up. To try to make sense of chaos is foolish. If you have been lucky enough to realize, 'Who Am I?' from an 'Absolute Scientist', revel in that! You are so lucky!!!

Whenever we look for pleasure of the five senses, we are beggars! We have infinite bliss and knowledge within us, why look outside in the relative world for physical and sensual pleasures? Our bodies are our temples. We live within them. The human body is extremely adaptable and natural. We are so caught-up in seeking pleasure of the five senses that we have become worse than four-legged animals in our blind quest! Life is not to be wasted away like this. We must live with some norms, limits and boundaries. Food is to be consumed for survival and nourishment. It is not something to obsess about. In today's world, people are constantly in search of 'fun'. What is fun? Fun is something that is frivolous, entertaining and stimulating to the five senses. Even children cannot learn unless the teacher is engaging and has creative methods to teach. Is this a disease? Every time we take ownership of a relative pleasure, we rob ourselves of the experience of the Pure Soul on the other side ten times over. We are drowning our experience of the Pure Soul with the salty seawater of the relative pleasures. Think about it. Why do people have hangovers? Why do people get depressed after a party or after having sex when they should not have done it? Or after they cheat on an exam or smoke a cigarette? They are seeking relief that is inherently unhealthy. Unhealthy breeds more unhealthy and then it compounds. The layers get thicker and thicker. The hole gets deeper and deeper. Let's start cleaning house now!!!

There is so much joy, peace, enlightenment and pure exhilaration in the Pure Soul. Let's not drown it out. It is such a free and beautiful experience. The simpler and plainer we become on the outside, the more joy and peace we will experience in our hearts. It is an oxymoron, it is ironic and it is profound. We must lose our selves in order to truly find ourselves. This is something that must occur naturally without any effort. Something only occurs naturally once there is complete understanding. After the understanding comes the real experience. Let's forge forward to that end.

Verse #37

"The Pure Soul possesses absolute bliss; Bliss boundless is not found in material things. The bliss boundless of the 'Real Self' is innately and naturally flowing bliss."

༄

Reflective Flashes—

We wake up in the morning thinking about all the backlog of the previous day or week. Our minds are clogged and our hearts are heavy at times with stress and confusion. This happens to us all. We have clogging in our pipes. Our karmic plumbing is not clear. We can utilize the tools of knowledge as Drano to clean these pipes. It takes effort and commitment to do this. Once these pipes are all cleared-up, then waking and sleeping will be all very normal and effortless. There will not be too much difference either way!

In this age of clash and conflict we must suffer silently and make our way out of this mess we created. There is no rhyme or reason to this madness yet it is all extremely exact in it's workings. The only seat worth claiming is that of the Pure Soul. It is a divine throne and should never be taken for granted. Cherish it, worship it and be one with it!

The Pure Soul will enable us to get out of even the worst of situations virtually untainted. There is so much power in seeing Pure Soul in other living beings that it cannot be stressed enough. There is a Pure Soul in each and every living being. Even someone who wants to kill you will turn back if we see his or her Pure Soul. They won't have the heart to go through with it. Our own purity protects us even in the midst of ambush and black mail. There are so many forces at work in our lives that we cannot even begin to imagine them! Our biggest obstacle is pointing fingers. If we learn to sit in the center and keep our File #1 as our best friend, we will find the answers and things will come to an amiable and neutral close.

One of the biggest mistakes in this life is to live to make others happy. This is not possible in this day-and-age. Live your life so you are as little trouble to someone else as possible. Strive never to be a burden to anyone. Other than that we do not have the power to make others happy. Happiness has to come from within. There is a myriad of mental, physical and emotional ailments that plague people that can only be cured by an Absolute Scientist.

Verse #38

"The worldly relative life is full of expectations; it goes on unraveling events incessantly; Take care of business as it arises with equanimity and poise."

❧

Reflective Flashes—

Money and status play such a tremendous role in the relative world. We judge people before they even have a chance to speak. We judge people by their background, their skin color, their clothes, their cars, their homes and even by the company they keep. It is so automatic and subtle that we sometimes do not even realize we are doing it. Our fragile egos and minds cannot bear the insults and subtle spitballs, which are, hurled at us daily. The world is our own projection. What is being received was petitioned for in the past. We must now be VERY careful that we do not bind new karma besides that which will free us from this awful bondage. The five divine dictates given to us by the Absolute Scientist are so powerful and their purpose is to help us cleanse our karmic slate in the next couple of lifetimes.

The two things that make the world go around are ultimately sex and money. People are driven by these two factors. It is sad but true. We must not allow ourselves to become slaves to either of these. Our goal is to clear the accounts. How can we clear the slates and be free from any obligation to anyone or anything? That is our goal on the path to liberation. When we die, we will not take money or people with us. We leave our mark and are on to the next life. Let's keep the load as light as possible for the next round. Even with this knowledge, it is most likely that there will be at least a couple of lives remaining. It is the nature of this clash-filled and antagonistic age that one life is not enough to clean house!

We must keep our minds clear with the power of prayer and the tools given to us by this Absolute Scientist. It is important to stay firm in our resolution to resolve each and every situation with equanimity within. Things may not always appear as though it was amicable and beautiful... the thermometer is within. We should not have any attachment/detachment or revengeful feelings once that event has passed. It is a temporary that has come and gone... we saw Pure Soul in all involved and we saw each as an innocent instrument including ourselves. If we an instrument to pain for another, we heartily repented, confessed and prayed for forgiveness to the Pure Soul of the afflicted. That is the science. It is THAT simple!

Things are rarely what they appear in this age of Kaliyug. People may be smiling, dancing and seemingly enjoying the company of their cohorts, however, on the inside may be loathing the very people they are with. This is an extremely complex age to be alive in. People are not one in their speech, thoughts and actions. They could say one thing, think another and yet do another! How complex is that? Do not try to figure it out... make your way out of this quagmire with the divine solution given by the Absolute Scientist. After all, it is all relative and temporary. Give people what satisfies their egos and move on. Let everyone take whatever they need to in order to clear the accounts.

Verse #39

"The deliverer of pain is merely an instrument, the fault is solely my own is to be fully understood. The vision & awareness of positive pure intention and vision is key."

☙

Reflective Flashes—

If we suffer, it is our fault. The pain in our hearts was delivered by us knowingly or unknowingly to others. That is why it is there. It doesn't compensate when we feel those sharp pangs of anguish in our hearts... but this is the cold, hard truth. We can soften the blow by forgiving ourselves first then forgiving the perceived perpetrators who are merely instruments or mail people delivering our requested mail to us.

Nobility and honor for the Pure Soul lay in taking ownership and accountability for our own pain. Furthermore, dealing with it in a positive and productive manner is our duty. We have the tools this knowledge provides us with to pour water on the raging fires within. We also have tools to spray water on the fires we cause in others. Use the heartfelt prayer tools such as repentance, confession and forgiveness requests from the Pure Soul of the afflicted. We can sing *Kirtan* to douse the fires within with the divine power of the Pure Soul. The key is the *heartfelt* part. We must be sincere in our prayers.

It does not really matter *how* we go about repenting with regards to language. What does matter is that it is sincere and untainted by any impure intentions. We may see things in our hearts that are not the prettiest things in the world. We may not want to see the black dots in our hearts, but they must be dealt with. Realize that any black marks in our hearts are usually caused by the pain and suffering we have experienced. With pure understanding and knowledge, we can wipe them clean. Do not ignore them! They will hinder progress on the path to liberation.

One of the best ways to counteract the negative emotions we experience when we see 'instruments' that have or continue to bring us pain is to picture ourselves putting a chandan bindi on their forehead, a garland of fresh jasmine flowers and washing their feet with our bare hands. This will immediately serve to re-channel the negative emotions and feelings to a positive and productive place.

Verse #40

"True knowledge is that which withstands the test of time & is evident at the time the situations arise; That which has been 'seen & known' can never be forgotten."

ৎ৵

Reflective Flashes—

IF we are in the center and connected to our Pure Soul and positioned on it's side, we are knower-perceiver. If not, we have failed the test examination. The Absolute Scientist only requires 60% for a passing grade. He only requires we stay within His divine dictates 60% of the time, and He will give us His divine protection and seal of approval for liberation within the next couple of lifetimes. This is not such a bad deal.

There are certain obstacles that are faced repeatedly throughout one's lifetime. These are hindrances we caused to others in the past and as a result are hindrances in this lifetime. When these situations arise, with the firepower of true knowledge, we can begin to dissolve these obstacles or hindrances. If we become entangled in the situation and fail to remain observer, then the opportunity has been lost. Nothing in this temporary world is forever. All things, emotions, people, relationships and events are to be known and seen for what they truly are.

The true test lies in when everything is going wrong, our level of strength, equanimity and patience in riding through the circumstances untainted internally. Our poise on the inside should remain unshaken! That does not mean we are not to take EVERY effort in the relative to avoid bad situations whether they be financial, personal or physical. This knowledge is not to be abused! That will result in things we do not even want to think about!

We must be careful not to judge and condemn others subconsciously. We can see-and-know the weaknesses for what they are but we cannot see them as being at fault. In our vision they must appear completely innocent as an instrument being guided by the forces of their own karma. Rise above those ingrained likes and dislikes! Demonstrate the world the power of this knowledge by living it every breathing moment.

Verse #41

"You are a victim of your own trap. You yourself are holding on to the
bondage. Let go of the steadfast grip on bondage and you will effortlessly
and innately be free."

ॐ

Reflective Flashes—

The bitter words we have heard in the past ring in our ears even 20 years
later! How sad that the human heart and psyche is so fragile. We cannot
seem to forget the pain inflicted on our egos, minds and emotions. The
human heart suffers blows that seem to be irreparable. We must move
on. We cannot allow bitter words to define our being. That is what we are
doing when we hold on to the past. It is dead. Let it go! The deliverer of
that pain or dish what a mere instrument. Do we keep reliving the pain in
our stomach after eating a bad meal? No. We move on. Why do we hold
onto these awful things? Human beings thrive on revenge in this day and
age. What is the saying? 'I don't get mad, I get even.' We harbor feelings
of wanting to bring justice. There is no injustice committed against you!
You yourself asked for all this. Why suffer double losses? Walk away
with whatever you have left. Be grateful for what you do have left and be
grateful the debt has been repaid. MOVE ON!!!
The bondage is primarily due to our relative ego. Our relatively projected
ego fights letting go of the past. The relatively projected ego likes to bring
justice. It is a sick game and we must rise above our petty egos and petty
minds. Once we realize that this game is only harmful to us and others, it
should help us to overcome the clinging to the memories of the past. Why
keep punishing ourselves and others with these memories? LET GO of the
past and embrace your Pure Soul in all it's power, grace, beauty and infinite
joy.
Remember the whole world is your customer or client in some way. You
have something to exchange with them whether it be positive, negative
or neutral. The key is to remember your fine line. Just as we keep our
professional lines in business we must keep our fine line at having the firm
intention of clearing the account even if it means losing in the relative.
When realize anyone we come into contact with or that encroaches our
space in our psyche, we must clear that account professionally like in
business.

Verse #42

"I alone am the root cause of all hassles', where this realization and exact understanding manifests; From 'that' place, all obstacles will effortlessly melt away."

❧

Reflective Flashes—

As the saying goes, 'It's all about me!' Well, it really is. It boils down to #1. What is your attitude? Do you appreciate what nature has provided you with? Are you 100% accountable for your actions and results? Or do you constantly whine and complain about how you were wronged? Do you point fingers and revel in self-pity? The negative attitude and negative outlook are the biggest obstacles to living a free and joyous life, even in the relative.

Each time we point a finger there are four pointing at us. It is impolite and unwise to point fingers. However, we continue to do this! It is too much work and too painful to see our own faults! It is so much easier to pass the buck. The longer we play the wrong game... the longer it will take to experience true freedom and joy. Be honest and unbiased with yourself. Be gentle but firm about-facing things as they truly are. Face your weaknesses and faults head on! That is the only way to rid of them. If you have knowledge, you are extra lucky! You have a free ride on the golden threshold of Pure Soul. It carries 'you' while your relative self must be perfected through careful scrutiny and observation. There are no free lunches in the relative, but the Absolute Scientist in all His grace and compassion, has given some of us a royal and blessed ride by placing us in the pedestal of Pure Soul. Infinite kudos and grateful regard to the Absolute Scientist!

We must find our place in this puzzle and find our way out of the maze by having and keeping a global vision. That can only be accomplished from the center. At the end of the day, we are responsible for ourselves. We must be accountable to everything and everyone in our lives if we want to attain freedom. Let's not kid ourselves! The debts of the past must be repaid. Enjoy clearing the account knowing that the end result will be eternal freedom. Smile in the midst of it all no matter how crazy or unbelievable the results may be. They were your own! You asked for every little thing in your life. Be aware and cognizant of what you feed into the impartial cosmic computer for the next round. Make sure it is going to lead to eternal freedom, if that is your goal. If not, you will only bear the fruits of whatever your sow. Choose to remove yourself from all the hassles.

Verse #43

"Obstacles are a reflection of one's own projections, you alone are responsible for them; Do not point any fingers, just grin & bear it gracefully."

꙳

Reflective Flashes—

We have no choice here in the relative. As it was wound, it will unwind. Our minds will con us into believing that we have choices... we were victims if it came out bad or we did it all if it came out great. In fact, we do not have the power to even blow a feather! We are completely powerless in this game of life. Our only source of power lay in our intentions, our convictions and our prayers. It is easy to find the greatest faults within us. All we have to do is see where our relative self encounters the most obstacles. The true penance lay in just grinning and bearing it knowing that it will pass as all temporary things do. Struggle and strife lead to blood shed. We do not want to see any blood anywhere. We are on a path of non-violence of the highest order. To the point where we do not assume doer ship at all! How deep is that?

There are times in our lives where nothing seems to go right. At every turn, there is obstacles and resistance. These are fruits of our wrong doings. These are results of the bitter seeds we had sown in the past. Let these times pass. If enough vision is there to see the causes, then use that opportunity to cleanse the slate through heartfelt confession, repentance and confirmation. Do not allow these times to pass without maximizing the opportunity for the Pure Soul. We must learn to think in terms of the benefit in the 'real'. For infinite lives we have been conditioned to think in terms of 'relative' profit and loss through the shadows and reflections of our intellect. We were conditioned to think in terms of relative profit and loss. Now, we understand that is not in our hands. What is in our hands is clearing the accounts with strong conviction, thus increasing our weight on the 'real' side. The scales have been so skewed for infinite lives in favor of the 'relative'. It is time to bring some balance!

Think of life like the last inning in a baseball game. We are pretty confident of what the outcome is going to be, however, we still play hard and strong till the end so we can end the game gracefully with respect and dignity. This is regardless of whether we won or lost. That is sportsmanship at it's best!

Verse #44

"If 'Who Am I?' is known, there remains nothing further to be accomplished; 'Knowing-seeing' alone will accomplish all that needs to be done."

∾

Reflective Flashes—

Everything in this world is relative that can be seen with the eyes, touched with the hands, tasted with our mouths, smelled with our noses and heard with our ears. The real does not have a speck of relative and vice versa. They run on two separate tracks! The benefit of knowing 'Who Am I?' is directly proportional to the confusion that arises in the relative of not knowing 'Who Am I?' We experience the anguish and pain in our hearts as a result of our past karma, however, once 'Who Am I?' is known, we learn to observe that pain, anger, pride, attachment and greed. Eventually, it exhausts itself and life becomes very 'dramatic' without anything touching us within our heart.

Therefore, at that point, we have learned to live in the royal seat of Pure Soul and identify with that as opposed to our relative self. Our relative self is really just a top that has been wound-up and is constantly unwinding until all the karma has been exhausted. So, knowing 'Who Am I?' really does solve the puzzle. It permanently quenches the thirst for the answer to the meaning of life. It all comes to a full stop on one side and the infinite is met on the other! What an adventure!

The beauty and miracle of this knowledge is that it truly places one on a pedestal and the work is done from the inside out. It is almost like a cocoon. The inner workings are going on and the beautiful butterfly that emerges is so unexpected and such a miracle! Who would have known? The difference is that the real is permanent and unfortunately a butterfly has a short life span but can be permanently preserved through our wonderful mounting practices in the relative world. Once we learn to think in terms of relative and real, the knowledge really begins to take off like a rocket towards space. This is difficult to achieve because of our conditioning from so many past lives. The knowing-seeing-perceiving aspect of Pure Soul enables the eventual transformation of the relative self to take place. Going back to the same concept of once a fault is seen, it disappears because it does not have the foundation of false identification to support it any longer. With the power of this knowledge, even the relative self is eventually transformed, thus the butterfly from an ugly caterpillar to a cocoon to voila!

Verse #45

"Freedom! Freedom! Want it now! When that fervor ignites within; the grantor of that will positively appear."

❧

Reflective Flashes—

Any developed human being that has reached a certain point in Maslow's Hierarchy of needs longs for and searches for freedom. Some attempt to find it through religion, spirituality, science or even witchcraft. The point is that most human beings are aware of the bondage, especially in this day and age. The problem is finding the right true liberator and guide to help one attain freedom.

In order to meet an Absolute Scientist that fervor must be very strong and distinct. The Absolute Scientist evaluates based not on the outside appearance or even behavior but the goods within. He looks at the heart of a person. How pure is that heart? How deep and wide is that heart? Does it have the potential to absorb this powerful knowledge and spread the light that it can ignite? Furthermore, does this person have the deep grasping power to understand this science in its entirety? Finally, how humble is this person?

An Absolute Scientist manifests on this earth only once in a million years. That is a long time! How valuable can this person be? It is not measurable. If you have been given the divine knowledge of the Pure Soul, do not discount the value or the power of what has been bestowed upon you. It is a great responsibility to be a Mahatma. That is not a title to be taken lightly. Allow your light to become a huge torch for this world that is truly drowning in darkness by staying within the five divine dictates that the Absolute Scientist has prescribed for us.

If you do not have this divine knowledge from an Absolute Scientist, make it your mission to get it! Make sure you know how to recognize an Absolute Scientist. He is so ordinary, humble and human in His dealings that only one that is truly in search of Him can recognize Him in all His greatness. The Absolute Scientist lives as the world's pupil. He is not out to achieve fame, fortune, or recognition. He is straightforward, extremely humble in his outward dealings and lives a life of simplicity and accountability to each and every living being that He comes into contact with. He is almost childlike on the outside. He is pure and does not have a speck of drive towards sex and sex-related activities. Good luck in your quest!

Verse #46

"When one's own faults can be seen that one absolutely attains the status of being 100% human or god-like; As a result, those faults will become baseless without a foundation to stand on ultimately perishing forever."

❧

Reflective Flashes—

Our own biases, inferiority complexes and prejudices give rise to fear and detachment. We engage in these based on our experiences. Modern psychology emphasizes the role of our childhood in the rest of our lives. If we were neglected or abused mentally, emotionally or physically, we tend to strive to make up for that by overachieving or giving up all together. If we did not get the attention we deserved, our being strives to attain it through either rebellion and/or over-achievement. These neuroses are not in our hands. They are a result of our own past karma. Through understanding and application of this science, these neuroses can be put to rest. The entire finger pointing mysteriously disappears and everything becomes very clear. That can take a while depending on how screwed-up we truly are! It is a hard truth to face, but this is personal fault. 100% our own doing whether consciously or unconsciously! What a slap in the face to face! As our practice becomes more promising in this Science of Absolutism, we actually will begin to enjoy seeing our 'own' faults. This is because 'we' are separate and the faults of our relative self once seen begin to disappear. Ultimately, our relative self is becoming closer and closer to being 'one' with the Pure Soul. In this crazy world where values, ethics and standards have basically turned upside down, this incredible science is extremely fitting. There is no other way to achieve liberation in this chaotic world. Yes, through discipline, prayer and penance, progress can be attained. However, without the knowledge of the Pure Soul, the ultimate goal is not attained.

Make it a goal to see at least 100 faults everyday. If this is not achieved, the day has been wasted. We set personal, professional and family goals so why not set spiritual goals? As more and more faults are seen, we will experience being lighter and lighter without the weight of the garbage! Life will begin to sail smoothly like a sailboat on a clear serene lake but with a steady wind to guide it in the right direction and beautiful scenery to be viewed!

Verse #47

"The whole world is in 'divine order', the master cosmic computer is perpetual and never stops; with this understanding, the false projection of ego subsides."

                                ॐ

Reflective Flashes—

When the relative self gets exhausted or tired, it is quite natural that doer ship can kick into place. If the relative self is not getting what it requires to stay balanced with regards to ego, affection, rest, and play, it will revolt! The ego then projects itself and causes uproar to occur in the hierarchy of the inner workings. The intellect will show the faults of others. The mind will generate all kinds of negative thoughts as a result. Additionally, the heart gets saddened and everything starts to break down internally. This breakdown will then impact the physical health eventually. This domino effect occurs often in this age of clash and conflict. It is all so scientific yet so difficult to grasp because all these dynamics cannot be seen with the human eyes. The beauty of this science and its divine knowledge is it has the power to break this cycle if applied correctly. Matter is physical, if it can be known for what it is exactly... many of these chain reactions can be intercepted.

Without the Absolute Scientist, true understanding cannot be obtained. Only the Absolute Scientist can bestow the correct understanding. He alone is equipped with the tools to accomplish this incredible feat. How difficult is it to move a mountain? That is what He is up against! And in all His humility and grace, He gives us this exact understanding in the palm of our hands. Without being given this divine understanding, it is impossible to understand. This is crucial to understand! Do we understand?!? A simple translation of this concept is that true understanding cannot occur without the Absolute Scientist. He alone can make one realize 'Who Am I?'

The anger, pride, attachment and greed that are expressed after obtaining knowledge from an Absolute Scientist are all discharge. Furthermore, the impact of that anger, pride, attachment and greed is softened considerably due to the light of the knowledge and presence of Pure Soul. This makes it a better world for all involved in that scenario. The Pure Soul of an unenlightened person will 'feel' the difference and it will cause a change in that person for the better. The false projection of ego does not go away but becomes 'dramatic' thus very light and relatively harmless to others.

Verse #48

"Live in & maximize the present, do not chase that which is not in the present; your entitlements will naturally meet-up with you."

❧

Reflective Flashes—

Most of us have come with so much excess baggage from the past lives; it truly is difficult to achieve this without the power of divine knowledge from an Absolute Scientist. He alone with the firepower of His divine knowledge can burn to ash the karmas from the past and lighten our load! He cannot relieve us from the karmas that are in the form of ice (figuratively speaking), however, the lighter karmas in the form of air and water can be completely zapped thus lightening our load! What grace and compassion He has in all His infinite wisdom!

When we are alone, our file #1 (relative self) is our main focus. We must keenly observe what is occurring in the mind, the reflective mind, the intellect and the speech and body. Also, we must observe any anger, pride, attachment and greed that come to pass as the mind, body and speech are discharging according to the universal cosmic computer's workings. The key is to maintain equanimity within and a firm conviction to clear the accounts with regards to one's own relative self. This requires us to be completely seated in the center with the Pure Soul. It cannot be accomplished in any other way! When we have other files around #2, #3, #4, #5 etcetera, we must allow our File #1 to interact with a firm intention to clear the accounts within us. If our File #1 revolts or behaves badly harming another's feeling, we must cajole and coax our File #1 into hearty confession, repentance and confirmation to the Pure Soul of that living being. Even a second is not be wasted in this lifetime.

This is a fact. This Science of Absolutism is not a religion or spiritual path. It is a fact of liberation! It is not a theory. It is a FACT. It is REAL. It alone can enable a human being to live in the present and not be obsessed/haunted with the past or worry about the future. When you are in your natural state, everything happens with a constant flow like the flow of natural spring water down a mountainside. It does not stop and contemplate what direction to take as it flows down a mountain. Its path is already carved out. Similarly when we are in the center, the relative self is as natural as a lion in the wilderness. Everything progresses instinctively and naturally.

Verse #49

"Flow with the present situation, stay far removed from friction of any kind; the essence of liberation is contained in this simple practice."

ॐ

Reflective Flashes—

How can we flow with the present situation? Adjust everywhere. Seriously! This is the only way. How can we adjust everywhere? Be a knower-perceiver. Be in the center planted firmly in the golden throne of Pure Soul. If we try this just one day of the week, we will see the incredible power of being a complete observer from morning 'til night. Everyone in the household will wonder what happened to you?! They will think some kind of miracle happened! Live in the home of your permanent home at all times. There is no better place. We know this.

Everyone is perfect in his or her own way! The world is so exact in all it's workings that it is unfathomable unless viewed from the center and with the exact knowledge bestowed by an Absolute Scientist. Relative is separate and real is separate. There is no crossing or connection of any sort except there is no relative without the presence of the real. However, there can be the 'real' without the presence of the relative. That, too, is only at the final destination where the living being has attained complete oneness with Pure Soul and no longer has to live in a body of any sort. Therefore, they are always parallel until the final destination has been reached. Even in the hellish states of being there has to be the presence of the Pure Soul. In the demi-god states of being there has to be presence of the Pure Soul as well. The plant and animal states of being must have the presence of Pure Soul without fault. And, of course, we know the human form must have the presence of Pure Soul in order to be. What makes the human form unique is that it is the only form from which karma can be bound. All the forms are complete discharge and natural. Once the existing karmas that created that being are exhausted, the universal cosmic computer will prepare that soul for their next birth according to their karmas from their past human life. So, the human life determines everything. How powerful is that? How important must this human life be? We cannot even begin to fathom! Let's STOP this sleeping with our eyes wide open!

Verse #50

"Lift those who have fallen, this is the main objective; ask not 'Why have you fallen?'"

∿

Reflective Flashes—

We cannot judge anybody for anything after obtaining this knowledge. This world is 100% innocent. We experience this fact through our experience of the Pure Soul. Our role as a Mahatma is a tremendous responsibility that is not to be taken lightly or treated nonchalantly. We are like God's police force. Our job is to protect, help and serve. It is our God given (literally) right to be instrumental towards the 'real' well-being of this world. We have no excuse! If a child makes a mistake and an adult makes the same mistake, aren't they treated differently? Aren't they held to different standards and codes of conduct? A child is forgiven for they know not. They are innocent. Does a mother scold a child if a child makes the same mistake as the mother? The mother knew better, therefore, should NOT have made the mistake, the child is innocent. This is a very simple example, however, as Mahatmas we are now in the role of the mother and all the living beings in the world are our children. Be not critical and judgmental of others. It is not our right to do this. We take tremendous risk of retribution from the laws of nature if we engage in this foolishness. We must be humble, encouraging and entirely tolerant with all the living beings of this world. These are all knowable. We need to only know and see what, when, how, why and who. We are like angels in human bodies for this world if we allow the knowledge to work through us and stay seated in the golden pure threshold of Pure Soul at all times. Furthermore, if we are instrumental in the bettering of others' lives, it is only 'instrumental'. We cannot take credit or develop a sense of pride about this! The knowledge was given to us instrumentally; therefore, any impact that occurs for others is by law also only instrumental. It would not work any other way! There would be no impact with false ego in the mix!

So, essentially, the more firmly planted we become in our seat of the Pure Soul, the more 'instrumental' we will be in this world towards the 'real' well-being of this world. Every single instance we stay firmly planted in the Pure Soul and see Pure Soul in another living being, we have expanded the light that we have been given by that much. The little candlewick needs to reach a point of being like an Olympic torch that will not and cannot burn out even in the worst of weather conditions! So, it is definitely to our advantage!

Verse #51

"Whatever the goods or merchandise may be within, surrender them all at the feet of the Absolute Scientist or Gyani; No longer are we filling our karmic bank with new goods or merchandise."

ॐ

Reflective Flashes—

We can think of this human life after obtaining divine knowledge from an Absolute Scientist, like a business. Do we want to run it cleanly and professionally or will we get sloppy, get a bad reputation, go out-of-business or worse, end up in lawsuits? In a business, whether a potential client buys from us or not, it is our goal to have an amicable and respectful interaction. The result may or may no be a sale. But, we do not want that person walking away and telling 10 people how horrible our business is and that no one should do business with us. Clean and professional is our goal!
I have had clients that have given me an earful for over an hour. What did I do? I just listened and quietly responded with a humble and sincere voice. It is a wonderful experience! As I was listening, I could see his Pure Soul and was definitely seated in the center! After the hour passed, he confided that I was a good person and my company was bad. I did not agree or disagree. I just listened! What else could I do! Furthermore, I prayed for his Pure Soul to attain some peace. He was obviously a disturbed person who was a recovering alcoholic. No body in this world could make him happy at this time.
So no matter what a client or potential client comes to get from our 'shop', our goal is to settle professionally and amicably without any recourse of any sort. How annoying is it to get court cases that go on and on and get appealed over and over again? That is definitely not our goal in any interaction in this lifetime. Isn't it a great feeling to really study for an exam and pass it the first time around? Our life is now a test examination. Every time we fail, we must take that test again at some point. The good news is that we have extra credit options! We can do hearty confession, repentance and confirmation to get it to passing level if done heartily. Aren't we lucky?

Verse #52

"In the obsession with worldly good & bad, there is an inadvertent disregard of nature's natural forces, in the external exactness of being Pure Soul is the 'real' renunciation; Let go of the worldly perceptions of good & bad by allowing things to happen without any friction or insistence on 'my way or the highway'."

જ

Reflective Flashes—

For the traditionalist this is very difficult to accomplish! It can only be done with the grace, compassion and direct link of an Absolute Scientist! He alone can free us from our concepts of bad and good. We were conditioned from a young age to believe certain things are 'good' and certain things are 'bad'. This is what our parents, aunts, uncles, teachers and other adults in our lives taught us to believe directly or indirectly. This leads to problems with this Absolute Science because according to this science, there is real and there is relative. This science is not a theory; it is fact. It is based on fact. The real cold hard truth that most people do not have the courage to face squarely!

In the relative terms, this almost sounds ludicrous! How can there be no good and no bad? Do we not follow laws and regulations? Are we not punished for wrong doings? Aren't criminals put to jail for committing heinous crimes? In the relative world, the answer is yes. However, according to the theory of karma, the thief who is enjoying his steal is not at fault. He is squaring the accounts. The one who is suffering without their belongings is a fault. The thief will have his squaring in the future depending on the intentions that he binds as a result of his actions. In other words, the fault lay with the one who is suffering. If we are suffering, it is our own fault! Deep down we all know this but do not live by it. If we learn to live by it, miracles will happen in our lives everyday!

If we are truly planted in the golden throne of the Pure Soul, the concept of good and bad, like and dislike, opinions and judgments begin to melt away like the ice on a rooftop with the heat of the sun beaming down upon it. We must put into practice this 'observation' of the happenings. It is a grand idea to engage in some practices that are directly against our relative self's nature to break some of these ingrained beliefs. If we are extremely miserly, force the relative self to shop at the most expensive store once in a while to wear that knot of greed down! If the relative self thinks the home will not run without them, take the relative self away for a few days. This will help this false sense of ego to dissolve! Life does go on without us! If the relative self has a low self esteem, take the relative self to a spa for some tender loving care. We can, through, understanding recognize and fracture our own faults through neutral observation, then strategic action. Just doing confessions, repentance and confirmation alone can work miracles. To the world, it appears that we are doing nothing special, but, in fact, those heartfelt prayers are moving mountains!

Verse #53

*"Forces outside of our realm have been called our own, it is a false belief;
with this understanding illusion will melt away & clarity will prevail."*

ॐ

Reflective Flashes—

We must learn to let go of this ego of doership. Nothing can happen
without so many evidences. For example, what do we need in order to
make a simple cup of tea? Even if we do not grate any ginger in it, we still
would need tea, sugar, hot water, a pot or heating container, a stove or fire,
a cup or two, a spoon or something to stir with! That is just a small list!
What about having the ability to drink the tea? Is this in our own power?
No! Not at all! We believe or super impose doership where it really does
not exist at all. We are like wound-up little toy cars... just spinning as we
were wound up! How sad. But, it is true. The only way we have any power
in our lives it through the realization of the Pure Soul. Once we know Pure
Soul and are separated permanently from our relative self then we live as
neighbors. We must make our relative self our best friend on this journey
to the ultimate freedom! We are eternally freed as Pure Soul, but we must
take the relative self to that freedom as well to be totally freed and fulfill
our mission in this universe.

When something happens according to our will. We boast about it and
how we did this or that to make it happen. Does anyone boast about losing
money in a bad investment? Does anyone boast when their marriage goes
south? Does anyone boast about having children that are not behaving
well? Does anyone boast about being a drug addict or alcoholic. Of
course not! Instead, they look for excuses and reasons to blame others,
circumstances and even God for their lack of success! If we renounce
ownership of the doership, then there is no illusion left. We are Pure Soul
and everything else is relative.

Clarity can only be attained when we are at the center of anything. When
we are professional with our clients and our intentions are in the right
place, everything stays clean and professional. Similarly, if we are in the
center as Pure Soul, we remain firmly planted and the relative self gets
the benefit of having clarity without the false projection of ego and it's
shadows! Those shadows that result as a by-product of the false projection
are the demons that haunt us! There is no joy or peace in illusion. Illusion
ultimately leads to destruction. Meaning it is relative and will perish just as
everything that is relative ultimately perishes. Only the Pure Soul is eternal
therefore God!

Verse #54

"To fix the broken glass, the Pure Soul does not have the power; there is infinite power & energy at the center (in the realm of the real)."

თ

Reflective Flashes—

If a glass or a plate breaks into hundreds or thousands of pieces, it is quite impossible for the average person to fix it. Only a professional glass blower could melt it down and recreate the piece. Also, this would not be a replica by any means! This is all in the realm of the relative. So, how does the Pure Soul in the realm of the real have infinite power? Why can it not fix the glass if it is so powerful? The Pure Soul's power is not of the relative realm. The Pure Soul can mend broken hearts, can help heal cracked minds and can fill emptiness in human beings with love and compassion. This is all done automatically. It is not something that it has to attempt to accomplish. Once a human being realizes Pure Soul, there heart and mind begin to heal just by the sheer light and power of the Pure Soul's presence. Yes, the Pure Soul does reside in every living being. But, if it is not realized, the impact is less dramatic. For a person who has not realized Pure Soul, the Pure Soul is there just to shed light in order for that projected relative self to live, just as a lamp lights a dark room. It is dormant light. If a person does not know the value of a diamond or cannot even recognize what it is, what good is that diamond to that person? It just serves as a cutting tool or something nice to look at! There has to be the eye of a true jeweler to recognize a real diamond. Similarly, when the Absolute Scientist gives the realization of the Pure Soul in the palm of our hands, it is up to us to be able to gage its value to maximize our benefit.

The human heart is extremely fragile and one of the purest parts of the body. We are extremely cautious in letting anyone take ownership of our heart. Most people are very picky about whom and to what degree they will allow anyone into their heart. We must allow our hearts to become an ocean that can even hold a place for our worst enemies. Then, the infinite joy and peace of the Pure Soul can truly be experienced. We can only accomplish this feat once we have become firmly planted on the golden throne of Pure Soul. The relative self then becomes just a by-product and we are eternal in our existence! Who does not want to live forever? Who is not seeking infinite life? If you have been given the realization of the Pure Soul, waste not a moment on the sidelines! Stay in the center! You will not regret it.

Verse #55

"There are no constants in the relative; the 'real' is eternally unwavering; from the standpoint of the constant & steadfast (seat of the Pure Soul) just 'see' all the fluctuating relative temporary things."

ॐ

Reflective Flashes—

There are no guarantees it the relative life. Anything can happen at anytime. It is all in the hands of foreign powers. There are so many beautiful and brilliant colors in nature. We could literally spend hours just gazing in awe at nature's beauty in some parts of the world. Similarly, the things that go on in the world are just shades of colors. They may not always be as beautiful as nature is! However, they are to be seen and known for what they are. If we are sitting in a train and we see a beautiful sunset on the water, we try to capture that picture in our mind so as to savor it! We do not need to get fixated on anything anymore, since what needs to be known has been known. If we have known Pure Soul, we have known everything! There is more beauty, brilliance and grace in the Pure Soul than even the most gorgeous sunset or beach. Some of the scenes we see and know in this lifetime pull at our heartstrings. They can make us somber. That is okay! It is the relative self that experiences that and we must know and see it.

What is meant by just 'see'? We must not get personally involved in the events occurring around us. It is important we direct our relative self to be sincere and appropriate in all the dealings with others. That is the relative self's duty and we are just to 'see' what, how, when and why the relative self behaves. If our relative self is out-of-line, we must make the relative self aware that we are opposed to that behavior, intent, thought or speech. It is our job to play the police. 'We' in the seat of Pure Soul are perfectly aware when something has not been cleared! The relative self feels the pinch in the heart and 'we' can 'see' that! It sounds complex, yet, after experiencing the separation is so simple and logical! It is difficult to digest because it is so perpendicularly opposite to the way we have viewed things for infinite lives! Just see the relative self in all the colors of the rainbow!

Verse #56

"You are bound by your opinions, give no opinions; stay steadfast as
'knower-perceiver' of all."

ॐ

Reflective Flashes—

Do we want freedom? Then the key is to let go of that which binds us! Our opinions bind us and give us those creases on our forehead. They give us our headaches and even some of our heartaches! How is it possible to live without forming opinions? Only in the pure royal throne of the Pure Soul can this be accomplished!

Our little minds are forming opinions constantly without us even be aware of it! The little dendrites in our brain constantly take different shapes as we change our opinions. It is a very dynamic process yet so subtle that most people miss it! We must be alert and aware in order to know the formation of opinions and the changing of opinions. It is ideal to be natural and unassuming.

In this world today people tend to be suspicious and untrusting due to all the scams that go on everyday. It is safer to actually rely on our instincts and our heart than our intellect. The intellect gives us information that is skewed by reflection. How does the sun's ray feel when they are direct vs. the rays that may be deflected off a wall or mirror? The feeling is very different. The heart and our own gut instincts are more accurate than relying on the intellect when faced with making decisions of trust.

If we take the time do some careful research we will realize how opinions are the chains that bind us! The ego is based on our opinions. We might think we are too good for certain 'kinds' of people. We might believe some kinds of people are bad or inferior. These are all chains that bind us because we have failed to validate the God within and instead have enforced our opinion! And sometimes we form this disdain on entire groups of people. Some people even detest animals such as cats and dogs. We are chaining are selves ludicrously by not validating the God within. These are outright violations of being 100% human. If we are 100% human, we understand that each and every living being has a Pure Soul and we respect that without question. There is not a need for opinions of any sort in that case. It is okay to have likes and dislikes that are of a normal nature. It is the degree of like and dislike that should not get elevated to a potentially threatening level.

Verse #57

"If wrong is known as wrong; the 'root' of the wrong will perish forever;
Wrong will become baseless without a foundation."

ᴄᴌ

Reflective Flashes—

In God's language wrong is anything that causes pain in any way to any living being. That includes anger, pride, attachment and greed. These are stronger weapons that hold more harming power than even punches, kicks and knives. The power of the tongue to inflict pain is greater than all the armies of the world put together. A single sentence can damage a child for life. A single statement can break a marriage of 30 years. A single thoughtless sentence can turn a person on the edge to suicide. Anger, pride, attachment and greed create atoms that are charged with that negative energy. That negative energy can pierce the heart of another living being. If we have knowledge from an Absolute Scientist, it is a tremendous responsibility if we impact others in this negative fashion. It is a direct opposition to the base and foundation of this Science of Absolutism. The consequences are grave. We alone face that responsibility. Even an Absolute Scientist cannot help us in that case.

On the flip side, a single word of encouragement can help an ailing person to heal. A single statement of love can turn a suicidal person away from the edge. The power of words cannot be stressed enough! Stifle the words that cause pain to others. Do whatever you need to in order to control the tongue! Reward yourself and others with thoughtful and cautious use of the tongue.

Our diet really does impact the quality of our mind, body and speech. We've all heard the saying, 'You are what you eat.' This is so true in the relative! Also, the relative directly impacts the quality of the 'real' experience. The ultimate goal is to attain complete 'oneness' with the Pure Soul. This can be accomplished by eating non-violent food. By eating food that has elevating and nutritious qualities, we lighten the load on the relative side. The goal is more soul power and less relative power. We need to put the scales in the favor of the 'real' by eating healthy, nutritious, light and, of course, pure vegetarian food. It is not necessary to eat till we feel like we are going to burst. A good balance is 1/3 solid food, 1/3 liquid and 1/3 air. Keep the tank 1/3 empty at all times to ensure alertness and awareness is at a peak.

Verse #58

" 'My' snares the 'I', without 'my' 'I' dysfunctions; Surrender 'I and my' at the feet of the 'Gyani' or Absolute Scientist."

ॐ

Reflective Flashes—

The first thing most people do each morning is mentally justify their existence on this earth. It happens quickly and most people probably do not even realize it is happening. It is an automatic assessment of where am I, who am I, what is the day going to be like, and is it great to be alive or not? If we have knowledge of 'Who Am I?', then this programming changes. We can greet our relative self in the morning! We can even ask, 'How was your sleep?' We are Pure Soul, the knower-perceiver and seer of all that the relative self experiences. Our existence is separate and eternal. This cannot occur without the grace of an Absolute Scientist.

Once we leave the relative self to perform his/her duties, it becomes less complicated. We are always there to guide, comfort and be there for our relative self, however, there is a lack of interference from excess ego that results from misplaced projection of self. The relative self is so much like a natural being (an animal) if left alone. This is not meant in a derogatory sense! It is just that the relative self is a natural product of our own karma and ultimately of nature. In order for us to experience complete separation after obtaining knowledge from an Absolute Scientist, we must practice the inner dialogue of relating to our relative self as a neighbor, as a completely separate entity. This inner dialogue will eventually lead us to have the upper hand with our best friend, the relative self. As Pure Soul, we have an energy called 'pragna' that works as our voice and authority with the relative self. The Pure Soul cannot speak! 'Pragna' functions to protect and uphold the Pure Soul and, at the same time, guide the relative self towards the Pure Soul, away from the temporary binding elements.

Once we have surrendered to the Absolute Scientist, we must hold strong in that decision. Really, what we have done is surrendered to the Pure Soul. Therefore, the battle is of the relative self. It's the relative self that surrenders and the relative self that fights the surrender at times. The old habits of infinite lives die hard! It is up to 'us' on our royal throne of Pure Soul to just 'see' the ups-and-downs of the relative self as purification slowly occurs. We are not giving away control by surrendering; we are taking the stand that is rightfully ours by complete surrender!

Verse #59

"The 'world' is known as 'fleeting', things come and go; Our time here is fleeting but a split second in the immense of eternity."

৵

Reflective Flashes —

This life is but a fleeting moment of time in the expanse of eternity! Why waste this precious human life? It is not worth wasting or losing a single moment. Our time in this body is limited. Lucky people get 80 to 100 years on this earth in their present bodies and most pass away between 60 and 80 years. Our problem is our egos. That is the root cause of all misery! Pain is inevitable, misery is our choice! Let's not kid ourselves, we give all our power to the ego. Ego controls everything we aspire to, dream of, cherish and loathe. Our egos are superimposed on a human animal that is at the mercy of nature, our relative self. By animal it means that the relative self is a natural being of nature without the excess of superimposed ego. All animals have enough natural ego to survive and function. Similarly, the relative self (human being) has enough natural ego without the false identification and superimposition of excess ego. This can only be applied with the knowledge of the Pure Soul. If we do not know where to place the real 'I', how can we let go of identification with the relative self? It would result in lunacy. We must have a place to park our ego or it is suicide.

We hear it all the time how precious time can be and how undervalued it truly is as one of the six eternals! It is not worth it to waste even a single moment! Once we have the diamond in the palm of our hands, there is nothing left to search out. We have it! It behooves us to know the diamond (Pure Soul) intimately from every angle. We must get our finest magnifiers and examining tools. For infinite lives we have known the relative things. Now that have the eternal, real diamond in the palm of our hand, we must scrutinize and examine to the finest details.
Let's maximize every moment in this human body. Our goal is to be instrumental in spreading peace, joy, light, pure love, guidance, non-violence and reverence for every living being. Our focus has changed from the external to the internal workings. What is really happening versus what we see and hear with our physical senses? The human mind and heart is as fragile as Mikasa glass and will shatter into thousands of pieces if not handled with utmost care.

Verse #60

"The relative is nothing but a snare in foreign powers, in the 'real'
seat of the Pure Soul there are no foreign powers; With this profound
understanding, stay firmly planted in the safe haven of the Pure Soul."

৵

Reflective Flashes—

This is so true! Every time we take a detour out of our safe haven, we
experience scorching! The world is seriously on fire. No matter where you
put your feet, it will be like stepping on hot coals. Even seemingly cool
places will have their bite after the fact! The key is to be non-involved. We
must maintain our position as knower-perceiver-seer of the circumstances.
We must 'see' what our relative self does, likes, dislikes, thinks, says, wishes
and experiences. This is a very subtle and deep concept that can only be
comprehended if the separation has occurred through the divine grace of
an Absolute Scientist. How lucky some of us are! We will realize the full
power of this knowledge as time goes by!
Where would we rather be? On a peaceful, beautiful, plentiful island or a
busy, smoggy, crowded and dangerous city? The choice is our own once
we have realized Pure Soul. It really is a no-brainer. The problem is that
we have been conditioned for infinite lives to identify with the relative
and acknowledge the real only when there is a crisis!   In the relative
there is always a loser and a winner in every situation. One man's gain
is another man's loss. There is always an equal and opposite reaction in
relative matters. It is scientific and unavoidable. On the other hand, the
real is always win-win because we are all of one quality. The Pure Soul is
all encompassing, constant and infinite by nature. We are all one by real
viewpoint. This can only be win-win regardless of what takes place in the
relative. Where would we rather identify ourselves?
There is only one place of permanent happiness. That is the seat of the
Pure Soul. There is no other place where permanent happiness can be
experienced or found. Every time we stick our feet or arms in the relative
realm 'personally' we are reducing our experience of the Pure Soul by that
amount. It is not worth the trouble by a long shot. It pays to stay firmly
planted in the seat of the Pure Soul!

Verse #61

"The root cause of all bondage is misplaced ego, if misplaced ego is renounced, freedom reigns; surrender your ego at the feet of the 'Gyani' or Absolute Scientist."

ॐ

Reflective Flashes—

By surrendering our ego at the feet of an Absolute Scientist, we are really taking on ownership of Pure Soul and our identification with Pure Soul. The Absolute Scientist is Pure Soul in human form. He has all the keys to open any lock! When we look at an Absolute Scientist, we see a mirror or reflection of our self. The Absolute Scientist is extremely light and humble by nature in the relative. He functions as a mirror or reflection for us in the relative world. While He is around, it behooves us to clean-up our act! Our ego is our worst enemy or best friend. It depends on where and how it is focused. Even without knowledge of the Pure Soul, if someone decides to live with the ego that they do no want to hurt any living being through their mind, body and speech, it is extremely beneficial on the spiritual path to liberation. It will at least allow that person to keep the human form. Each and every living being is in search of permanent happiness. How can it be accomplished while believing yourself to be someone you really are not? We hear the cliché, 'Just be yourself,' all the time. How can you be yourself if you do not know who you are? Yes, the relative self is much happier when there is no struggle and strife. The relative self needs room for self-expression and natural progression through life. That is a relative thing!

The mind is the next challenge after ego. The mind can drive us nuts! It will keep generating new thoughts, unwanted thoughts and ideas that will get endorsed by the intellect and ultimately end up affecting our ego! What a sad vicious circle! Once we are aware of these inner workings, the power of this parliamentary internal government is greatly reduced. It becomes manageable because it is a 'known' rather than a influencer. While we are identified with the relative, everything influences us. The mind, intellect, speech, thoughts, and ego all play their games with us. However, once they become a 'known', the power is gone. 'We' are separate as knower-perceiver-seer of all of these.

Ah, the freedom and bliss of knowing, 'Who Am I'! May everyone in the world have the fortunate karma to meet up with an Absolute Scientist and recognize Him in all his humility and grace as the enlightened horn of plenty He truly is!

Verse #62

"If you are the doer, then you are the defendant, the non-doer cannot be a defendant; the pre-recorded impartial cosmic computer software energy (vyavsthit shakti) is the instrumental doer."

☙

Reflective Flashes—

In a court case there is usually a plaintiff (accuser) and defendant (accused) and attorneys for both. The judge is the main facilitator and controller of the environment. For our purposes, the plaintiff and defendant are both our relative self. If we are suffering we are at fault so we would be the plaintiffs in that instance. On the other hand, if we are being accused, we are the defendant that is innocent until proven guilty. The beauty of this science is that it acquits us of all our crimes whether we are accused or not! We are not the doer! This is deep and sounds a bit ludicrous. It must be kept in context of the Science of Absolutism and it's foundation. This science cannot be misused! There are grave consequences if we misuse this knowledge. It is only considered the workings of the impartial cosmic computer software energy AFTER we have made every effort in the relative. This is NOT a license to live recklessly and without any responsibility. In fact, once we have knowledge there is the weight of tremendous responsibility on our shoulders as we KNOW. Aren't the consequences different if an adult who knows better commits a crime versus a juvenile? Similarly, we are considered the adult that knows better because we know 'Who Am I'! Nature punishes ignorance with a lighter sentence than the crimes done with knowledge. Our criminal justice system was created with great thought and care from intelligent human beings who sought to keep it as fair as possible. So the real freedom is not from responsibility from one's actions, but from knowing and understanding who the real doer is. 'We' must be responsible and keep our relative self in line. If the relative self steps out-of-line, then heartfelt confession, repentance and confirmation must be done. We are the police of this process for our relative self. Ultimately, it is our way of clearing our account with our relative self by keeping the slate clean! Wow! What clarity there truly is with the Science of Absolutism.

Verse #63

"If the rope gets knotted, don't tug on it, firmly and sincerely resolve the universe to straighten it out; the solution will surely arrive."

❧

Reflective Flashes—

Just as you can take a horse to water and cannot make it drink, we must not have unnatural insistence and doggedness about fixing things that are apparently broken in the relative. Whether it is a relationship, a personal problem, a bad habit or a major conflict with the authorities, we must first sit down and pray heartily. The prayer is directed to the Pure Souls of those involved and towards the evidences that are involved. Our resolve and heartfelt prayer is that things will work themselves out amicably with no pain to any living being. Pain is inevitable but misery is not. Our goal and conviction is that we want to settle the account without any pain to any living being. If any living being due to our involvement with them experiences pain, we must heartily perform confession, repentance and confirmation to the Pure Soul of that living being. In other words, our activities for solving problems are not on the outside. They are internal. There is more power in the activities of the inner self than of the relative self. The relative self is a top that spins and unwinds according to how it was wound.

By being in the center as Pure Soul, we have officially renounced the relative. The relative is incidental to our existence. The temporary is just that and we are now permanent. It is very beautiful as it is! Let's take all of our glasses and contacts out of our eyes and see things just for what they are!

It is not beneficial to focus heavily on relative solutions. If someone gets ill, we must consult with the doctor. That is relative. If someone gets robbed, a police report must be filed. That is relative. The real work is seeing the Pure Souls of those involved, engaging in heartfelt prayer and conviction. That is the 'real' work. There is relative and there is real in every situation. They are totally separate. Learn to recognize and be cognizant of 'real' and 'relative' in every life situation. Make a journal, draw a line down the middle and in every 'situation' as it arises record the relative versus the real. What is it that we truly are understanding? What do we see? This is an extremely important exercise in the Science of Absolutism. If we do not do this, we are cheating ourselves!

Verse #64

"The one who loses (with 'real' understanding) in the foreign realm of the
relative world, that one will be safeguarded from accidents; that blessed
one will surely and effortlessly absorb the eternal essence of the Pure Soul."

ॐ

Reflective Flashes—

In God's language, the one who lives with the least conflict and clash in
their lives is a winner! That blessed one will probably hear words like
pushover, spineless, wimpy, sissy and others that are not worth mentioning!
However, eventually that one will come out ahead! How? Nature, the
demi-gods/goddesses (saints or angels), even friends and family will want
to help that one get whatever he/she wants in life. The leadership is subtle
yet extremely powerful. That one will have any army of souls rooting for
him/her.

The laws of nature are counter-intuitive to human nature. Human nature
is to find a way that is against the tide, to find fault, to question and to
want more at all costs! This is particularly true in today's age of clash,
conflict and chaos. The ultimate goal is to be so lost in the Pure Soul that
the relative things become like watching a movie completely detached
and removed from any emotion. Of course, the relative self plays the part
perfectly but it is all 'dramatic' only.

What does it mean to lose in the relative with 'real' understanding? Well,
if there is a client who provides more than 40% of our business and of
course we do everything in our power to retain that client; however, the
client still is lost. It must be understood that the client was not truly ours
to begin with! There was no loyalty in the relationship. We must sincerely
and honorably let it go and move on to the next potential client. That is
losing gracefully with 'real' understanding in the relative. Another example
is if we would like to marry a certain person and there are several other
individuals who also would like to marry the same individual. Do we fight
for that person? Is it worth fighting over? No. We make our best effort
and move on. That is losing with 'real' understanding. Also, if we have
parents who do not notice us and care for us according to our expectations,
is it wise to sever the relationship or commit suicide over it? No, 'real'
understanding allows us to gracefully lose in the relative and receive so
much more on the other side.

Verse #65

"The intentions with which karma has been wound, it will unravel with the same; to wind (bind) karma with 'real' understanding is our only own 'real' power."

જ

Reflective Flashes—

Everyone wants power and control whether they admit it or not! It is human nature to want power and control. Why do people become drug and alcohol addicts? They seem to think they are in control because it makes them feel like they are in control when they take drugs or drink alcohol. By the time they discover how destructive it is, it is too late! They have already become chemically dependent. It is like being between a rock and a hard place once they are addicted for everyone involved in the situation! If they wish they had never started and repent, they will not do it in their next life. And if they really create a strong conviction and ego to quit, they may just actually kick the habit in this lifetime. It all depends. The point is that they feel powerless and out-of-control so they turn to these vices. In this age of clash and conflict, it is easy to feel like we are driving a car that does not have any controls! It is the nature of our collective karmas!

Someone could have the most noble intentions for their children, yet if the karmas were not bound in that manner; the outcome may appear the opposite! However, at the present moment the intentions are pure and positive! How sad! Do we not see this everyday in these dysfunctional and broken homes? It is scary that none of the outcome is in our hands! With the power of knowing Pure Soul, the load can be greatly lightened and even at times changed. This requires intense and heartfelt conviction and prayer on the part of the individual wanting the outcome to be different! When there is a will, there is a way! We must turn to the power of prayer and the God within.

The knowledge of Pure Soul can transform the most negative pessimistic person into a positive thinking human machine!

Our intentions as people on the path to liberation is to clear the accounts! That is our sole aim. Therefore, the goal is clear and simple. Yes, as we learn what helps and hinders on the path to liberation for the relative bound self, we change our intentions with regards to eating, sleeping and other habits to help maintain steadiness and strength in Pure Soul. In other words, our intentions are all surrounding attaining complete oneness with Pure Soul!

Verse #66

"No matter how darkness is sliced or dissected with the immense power of our minds; Not a single ray or glimmer of light can be found."

✺

Reflective Flashes—

When we are immersed in the darkness we know it! We cannot see straight! We think we can but in reality everything is distorted. Darkness is a black hole that has no end. It goes to the core of the earth's mantle. It is not a pretty place. None of us like to be there but we have all been there at some time or another. Some have been there more than others. It is the ugly side. It is the negative side. It is the destructive side. It is the spiritually suicidal side.

The Absolute Scientist has informed us in all His divine compassion and grace, that suicide is the one thing that really leaves it's horrible mark. Someone who has committed suicide will have thoughts of suicide and may commit suicide for the next seven human lives. What a curse! Thoughts of suicide are darkness. Thoughts of hurting others are darkness. Thoughts of revenge are darkness. Thoughts of stealing are darkness. Thoughts of cheating are darkness. There is no light there. It is up to us to lift ourselves out of the darkness through prayer and conviction. We must earn the grace and compassion of the Absolute Scientist and He will lift us out as well. Darkness is when we cannot see our own faults. Unfortunately, most of the world lives in darkness. Seeing our own faults is something that can only be accomplished with the grace and compassion of an Absolute Scientist who humbles us and enlightens us with our true identity. When we are in the dark, our path is not lit in any way. The puzzle is so chaotic that it cannot be solved. When we lose sight of our goals, it is darkness. When we get consumed with hatred and frustration, it is darkness. When we value the wrong things, it is darkness. When we cannot and will not forgive, it is darkness. When we will not pray and acknowledge the God within every living being, it is darkness. When we live only to satisfy our five senses, it is darkness. When we engage in self-hatred, it is darkness. When we fail to be positive, it is darkness. Quite frankly, there is more darkness out there than anything else! It behooves us to be as positive as possible so not only will be make the world a better place but we will attract more positive people to us. It is all magnetic. Do we want our charge to be positive or negative? Do we want to emanate optimistic or pessimistic? The choice truly is our own.

Verse #67

"The divine blessing of hardship, awakens the 'real' endeavor for the infinite knowledge of the Pure Soul; it is a divine 'vitamin' for the benefit of the Pure Soul."

❦

Reflective Flashes—

It cannot be said that I have not had enough bitter pills to swallow in my lifetime! Okay, let's all play our little violins! Most of us in this bitter and scathing age have had our fair share of bitter pills to swallow. When we realize all these 'instruments' that were 'instrumental' in our sorrow and pain are innocent, it sure does lighten the load! They were just playing their part in the song that the conductor was commanding. Oh, what a relief! It was not anything personal at all! Does it pay to be angry and upset with God? Well, once we have realized, God is within us and every living being out there, that does not make any sense either? So, where to direct all that rage? There is the productive practice of re-channeling that tremendous energy into something positive and helpful to oneself and others through prayer and worship of God.

Once we learn to view problems, trials and tribulations as challenges and divine vitamins for the Pure Soul, life becomes for manageable. It actually makes more sense. Everytime something or someone upsets us, we know we have stepped-out of the center. We return back 'home' to our haven of Pure Soul where infinite joy, knowledge, energy, vision and peace reside. It sounds corny but it functions like a silent alarm system for protecting the interest of the Pure Soul. The unpleasant and unwanted keeps us from straying too far away from the center. We have done this for infinite lives so it is easy to stray, however, with the 'vitamins' of unwanted and unpleasant events, we come back to the center. Imagine what it is like for those who do not know where and what the center is. This is why we must have unhindered compassion for the world around us. Not everyone is fortunate enough to meet an Absolute Scientist let alone obtain the knowledge of Pure Soul from Him.

No matter how pretty things look from the outside, there are always the wonderful 'bitter' vitamins to keep us clear of any fog of illusion. It is kind of like a laxative. It keeps our system clean from the waste of false belief and illusion. How grateful and thankful we are for the 'bitter' pills life serves us! They have become a blessing rather than a curse! Otherwise, how would we break the habits of infinite life times?

Verse #68

"Both pleasure & pain are shrouds of temporary circumstances; from a distance simply 'see' the happenings."

❧

Reflective Flashes—

As we develop a practice of being firmly planted in Pure Soul, we will serve as a mirror for the world. If someone is agitated and it does not affect us at all, we can be sure that we have served as a mirror for that person. We have done nothing to agitate that person; yet, they are agitated at seeing us! We are completely unaffected by their demeanor. In that instance, we are firmly planted in Pure Soul and that person has no effect on us. We are simply functioning as a mirror for them. It behooves us at that point to say a prayer for their Pure Soul and move on!

The 'real' and 'relative' are truly TOTALLY separate. We may be experiencing tremendous joy and peace within yet on the outside any normal person would not be able to tell. This is because our joy and peace is due to the 'real' connection so it is not visible in the ordinary relative life. This is directly in line with the Science of Absolutism. The relative self could be shedding tears and 'we' as Pure Soul remain knower-perceiver. The relative self could be laughing and joking in the relative and 'we' as Pure Soul remain knower-perceiver. The relative self could be arguing with a loved one and 'we' remain as Pure Soul knower-perceiver. In that instance, 'we' can see the Pure Soul of the one with whom our neighbor (relative self) is arguing. In this case, 'we' must ask our relative self to engage in confession, repentance and confirmation with the Pure Soul of the other person. It is all very structured and logical! It takes a little getting used to!

When 'we' feel everything is out-of-control, it is likely 'we' are in the wrong seat. In the seat of Pure Soul, everything makes sense. Even strange and crazy happenings and people, do not shock us because 'we' are centered. People talk about being 'centered', however, do not know the true meaning of this concept because they still believe the projected image of karma to be themselves. They even may 'get it' for a brief moment when life humbles them, however, cannot stay in that spot for very long for they do not know Pure Soul as their true identity. We must have the utmost compassion and humility with those who do not have knowledge of the Pure Soul. It is our duty to help them to reach higher planes spiritually by seeing their Pure Soul.

Verse #69

"The antithesis to action is simply reaction; by the workings of nature this continues to occur; Nature is in it's own exact order."

⚜

Reflective Flashes —

The only rhyme or reason we can attribute to all this chaos is our own blunders and mistakes from past lives. Just imagine if the President of the United States believed himself to be a monkey or tiger instead of a human being who is leading one of the most powerful countries in the world! We sincerely believed ourselves to be the person we were in our past lives. This led to some serious binding of karma. It is the law of nature. If we accidentally put our hand in fire, will it burn? Yes. Through our own ignorance, we have created this reality that our relative self lives today. We might think to ourselves, 'What a mess!' Well, that just confirms the level and degree of ignorance we were trapped in to be binding the kind of karmas we see the result of today. Do we have any choice now? Well, we do not have any choice in the result. But we do have the ability to control the new software that is being written. Will it be software that frees us or binds us further? That is up to us individually.

What about President Reagan? At one time he was the President of the United States and today he cannot remember who he is! This is the nature of the relative. It is constantly changing and so unpredictable. The results can be so drastically opposite in the same lifetime. This is all foreign department. It is not in our hands! If it were, would Ronald Reagan put his wife through what she is enduring? Probably not! Regardless of how we try to convince ourselves that we are in control of the relative, we will ultimately be proven wrong. Do you think Mahatma Ghandiji ever thought he would be assassinated the way he was? He was the instrument to India's freedom, however, his destiny was to die in this manner. He did achieve fame and reverence for many years to come.

Nature is extremely exact. Every atom, molecule and the minutest of particles is within the exact laws of nature. Just as a software program runs exactly as it is programmed, the scientific circumstantial evidences come together as they were programmed by the karmic cosmic computer. The actual framework of the software was in the form of intentions, wishes, convictions and passions of people. The creation is in the hands of nature 100%.

Verse #70

"The whole world blames the 'instrument' the faulty one roams free; nature ultimately catches-up with the wrong-doer & brings natural justice."

ॐ

Reflective Flashes—

This sounds ludicrous upon first reading! What do we mean that the world blames the instrument? Is the thief who steals not at fault? Yes, in the relative sense, but no in the 'real' sense. From a 'real' perspective, the thief is an instrument or postman delivering the results of the accuser's past karma. The accuser had in their past life stolen, supported someone stealing or caused someone to steal to have a thief steal from him/her today. This knowledge is to be understood by the one who has suffered the loss. The fault lies with the one who is suffering today.

It is crucial to remember that we must still file a police report even though we have this knowledge because that is normal and customary in the relative. This knowledge is for our own benefit within. It is not to be broadcasted or voiced in the relative world.

The one who has committed the crime may or may not be binding negative karma depending on his/her intentions. The thief who steals just so he/she can survive and wishes that he/she did not have to do it and repents for it will not steal in his/her next life. However, if the mentality is that 'I am such a great thief', then there is the seeds for stealing again in the next life. The interesting thing is that there is nothing personal in the events. The events are connected only by their impact on the individuals involved. The karma and it's binding is all very personal to the individual. Half the battle is realizing the world is our own reflection. A reflection of what we projected in the past! The fallacy with what people believe today is believing we are projecting what we create now. No, it is actually what we sowed in the past that is being projected now. It is so subtle and deep yet so simple once it is grasped! The core wrong belief is that 'I am this person'. So, depression is rampant because there is so much inconsistency in behavior, standards and ethics in today's world. People get depressed because of their own thoughts and behaviors! They can see how skewed and inconsistent it is yet cannot separate themselves without an Absolute Scientist to put them in the seat of their Pure Soul. How sad!

The beauty of being in the center as Pure Soul, 'we' are no longer the accused or the accuser. 'We' are separate as observer, knower-perceiver only.

Verse #71

"Whatever the pre-recorded impartial cosmic computer energies of nature have programmed, that alone will prevail; No living being can be spared from the workings of this exact impartial energy."

ॐ

Reflective Flashes –

The result cannot be changed. Is it possible to change a movie as it is playing on the screen? It has already been encoded onto the microfilm and the projector has already been started. The only thing that we can do is leave the theatre or close our eyes and ears. There is no escape! If the company that is with us will be upset, we cannot leave even if we really do not like the film! What about the actors and actresses in the film? Can they wipe themselves out? No. It has already been played out and programmed. It is better to keep our eyes and ears open. Be alert. And focus on the most positive aspects of the film whether we are in a lead role or are not playing a role at all. It is all to be seen for it cannot be tampered with! This is a very deep and subtle concept. It cannot be understood fully with the indirect light of the intellect. We must truly be seated in the center as Pure Soul to digest this concept. The heart can accept it but the intellect will by habit continue to fight it!

No living being can be spared from the working of this exact impartial energy means even ants, microorganisms, birds and pets are synchronized with the power of nature's energy. Every single living being in the universe is driven by this impartial energy and none can operate outside of this energy. Where does the energy come from? It is a product of our own desires, dreams, visions and intentions. We, as humans, cause nature to have to produce the things we see. The rampant growth of technology is not a coincidence. Humans have gotten lazier and have dreamt of creating and using jets, sports cars, computers and digital cameras! So, the impartial cosmic computer has to produce the software in the form of scientific circumstantial evidences that causes this to actually occur. Humans are just one of the instruments but due to ego believe themselves to be the ones making 'it' happen! Why have we had heated battles over 'intellectual property'? It is a sickness and disease that once again humans created due to ego. Actually, we are the root cause, but the execution is not of our own doing! How sadly twisted our beliefs have been for infinite lives!

Verse #72

"Natural human tendencies are myriad like the flowers in a universal garden, each blossoms at it's own time & space; with a myriad of shapes, colors & styles."

ॐ

Reflective Flashes—

Each living being lives according to their own time, space and karma. No matter how one tries to analyze this behavior through the intellect there will always be imperfections. We cannot make assumptions about any living being in this universe! They themselves are dependent on foreign powers and we, too, are at the mercy of foreign powers in the relative. We bound the karma believing ourselves to be the relative and now we wonder why everything is the way it is! What a mess!

Once 'we' are in the center as Pure Soul, all falls into it's appropriate place. We see the relative world and the 'real' world for what they truly are! The 'knowables' become infinite! There are so many flavors of personalities. Each has it's own proportions of sugar, spice and cinnamon. In some cases, there are some personalities that also have the bite of bitter melon and salt. Rather than viewing the faults of others, our ability to segment and separate the real from relative allows us to know relative personalities from a neutral standpoint. This is extremely powerful! It can transform even the most antagonistic personality within minutes! Even if there is no transformation, the element of effect on us internally is null and void! If it is not null and void, then our relative self must search for the fault that caused the effect and remedy it with the appropriate medicine (confession, repentance and confirmation to the Pure Soul of that person).

The prism of color has infinite shades. Similarly, the relative self has infinite flavors of personalities. There are four basic colors that dominate personalities. There is the red personality that is expressive and tells others what they feel and what to do. There is the green personality that is a driver and also tells people how it should be done. There is the blue personality that is mostly amiable and wants to please everybody. Finally, there is the yellow personality that analyzes everything and is not overly emotional in their dealings. These are generalizations, however, there is combinations, hybrids, different shades and the possibilities are infinite of where any particular person may fall within these four basic colors!

Verse #73

"The circumstances that are encountered should be met with a clear & free mind; it is crucial to get free from the web of our own karmic bindings."

ॐ

Reflective Flashes —

This is so easy to say and when the opinions of the past result in emotions with anger, pride, attachment and greed; it seems like everything becomes clouded! However, if our intention and conviction is strong in that we want to get free, the power of Pure Soul will remain stronger than the forces of the foreign substances (relative effects of karma). If 'we' are firmly planted in the center and 'we' can see all the knowable including our relative self, internally 'we' remain untouched and steadfast in the seat of Pure Soul. Each and every circumstance we pass through after knowledge is a test. If we fail, we will undoubtedly have to go through it again. Our mission each morning is to clear our accounts with each and every living being we encounter.

It is simple yet our complex minds make it complex and confusing! The intellect is one of our worst enemies if not steered in the correct direction. 'We' need to coax the intellect in our favor on the path to liberation. This is no easy task! The grace and compassion of an Absolute Scientist definitely helps.

For every perceived happiness in life, there is on the other side the counterbalance of unhappiness. When a child is born, another couple is experiencing pain because they cannot have children. The family with the newborn child is celebrating the birth and their joy knows no bounds. On the other hand, the couple that has tried everything to have a child but is unsuccessful is frustrated and angry. People with healthy minds will think of the positive alternatives such as adoption. But, at the end of the day, even an adoption is still pain for another living being! The millions of children without families would remain unfulfilled. Not to mention, the pain that the original parents of the child may be enduring. Bottom line, in the relative world, for every gain there is a loss and vice versa. There is no such thing as a true win-win in the relative world. Our intellect will show us these scenarios and justify things as win-win, but those are all games. The only true win-win is settling the accounts and bringing the balance to zero with each and every living being in the language of the Science of Absolutism.

Verse #74

"Circumstances are just the workings of the pre-recorded impartial energies of a cosmic computer software, meet and deal with circumstances in a spirit of equanimity; With complete understanding of the fleeting & transitory nature of circumstances or happenings."

وي

Reflective Flashes—

A spirit of equanimity involves strength, willpower, understanding, clarity and purity. We must live our lives with clarity of purpose and vision. Unless we hold ourselves 100% accountable in all situations, this will not be possible. 100% accountability involves 100% responsibility. This also leads to the conclusion that we cannot be 100% (or even close) in either of these categories unless we are non-doer. If we are non-doer then we are Pure Soul. Ultimately it all leads back to the center!

Unfortunately, in this age of clash and conflict, for every sweet morsel we taste, we will get smacked with a 100 bitter shots! It is a blessing in disguise because that helps us stay in the center rather than get lulled into the illusory world of relative projections!

One of the things that no one can stop is time. Time is it's own boss. Time is an eternal. It cannot be captured except by video or camera. Time passes whether we want it to or not! Similarly, the Pure Soul is permanent. It is the constant amidst the craziness. If we stay firmly planted in the golden seat of Pure Soul, everything else is a film to be seen including our relative self.

How long does it take to recover from an awful movie? It can be an hour, a day, a few days or a couple of weeks at most. If 'we' are Pure Soul, then the recovery is only for the relative self. The relative self is continually regenerating cells and in the process of input and output mentally, emotionally and physically. These processes are to be observed and studied carefully. 'We' must learn to thoroughly know every aspect of the relative as well as the real.

The quest for liberation is a diametrically opposite one to the ways of the world. Probably over 99% of the population on the earth consumes meat. Meaning that that we are not a large group! Meaning those that truly practice and live a life of non-violence even in the relative. We are few but proud. Make it count for all it's worth!

Verse #75

"To take the position of identifying with & upholding the temporary self is the ultimate risk; to identify with the Pure Soul is eternal truth."

જ

Reflective Flashes—

Even in the relative world without knowledge of the Pure Soul people talk about being honest with oneself and being accountable for one's attitudes. This is not something people are unaware of! It is sad that most people realize there is something permanent about them but do not know what it is exactly. They can feel there is something like a soul but don't know exactly what is permanent and what is relative. This is exactly what the Absolute Scientist enables people to understand.

Once we have knowledge of Pure Soul, it is spiritual suicide to take the position of upholding and defending the relative self. The relative self is temporary. We must come clean in order to be one with Pure Soul. Otherwise, it is all in vain. Even with knowledge of Pure Soul, it is wasted if our loyalty is to the relative self. Our position of loyalty must be 100% for the Pure Soul. Our thirst must only be quenched with the nectar of Pure Soul's juice.

However, it is important to play our role in the relative without flaw. The world will not let you go without getting what you owe and receiving what you have in your account balance. It is a paradox, however, so simple if we know 'Who Am I' in its exact sense. Without the Absolute Scientist, it is not possible to know, 'Who Am I'. The key in the relative is not to shelter or protect the faults of the relative self. We must protect our first neighbor from any harm, but not help conceal and uphold the relative self's faults. The faults must be revealed and exposed fully so the can be extinguished forever.

One of the thermometers within to test if we are in favor of the relative self is the level of anticipation within that we feel for any relative situation, activity or gathering. Is there a 'sweetness' felt within? Is there a juice of 'sweet' anticipation? That is the 'sweet' stickiness that does not allow complete separation and focus to remain in that particular situation. We must be aware where there is attachment and anything related to that attachment.

For parents, the children are a very large factor of attachment. If someone praises our child, we feel those 'sweet' juices flowing. If our child tells us how much they love us, we feel those 'sweet' juices flowing. Beware!!

Verse #76

"One who is cautious with words will experience inner freedom (mukti); if no one is querying, it is wisest to remain silent."

و

Reflective Flashes—

Wisdom is something that cannot be captured by the intellect. It is something we justify with our intellect but the true essence of wisdom is only demonstrated through the living example of one who is truly wise. We can learn from observation that is free from opinion. This is true of an Absolute Scientist. We can learn from observing and digesting the 'behavior' both external and subtle in order to 'absorb' the same wisdom. We will only assume as much wisdom as we are able to see with our inner eyes.

There is a saying that sometimes 'silence' speaks much louder than words. This is profoundly true. It must be an educated silence to mean anything. It cannot be a silence borne out of spite, revenge, anger or resentment. It must be a silence that is spiritual and pure in order to have a profound impact. The intent behind the silence is key.

Words have power. They are a form of energy in the cosmic impartial computer of the universe. They are charged with either positive or negative energy. Furthermore, there is opinion and intent behind words. Words can be extremely hurtful once they leave our lips and our heard. It is safer to stay quiet if we are not aware of the impact our words can have on another living being. What words can bring comfort to parents who have lost an 18-year-old child to a car accident? There are not many words that can comfort at such a tragic time in someone's life. Our silent prayers will speak much louder at these difficult times.

If we can exhibit a little caution, restraint and humility prior to using words with any living being, our lives will be transformed. Our spirituality and presence can grow exponentially. The key is awareness and alertness. If it helps to count to five or utter a brief prayer prior to speaking, that is a helpful habit. Find a way to exhibit some control with speech and it will have a significant impact on the quality of our lives, our family life and our impact on our community.

Why waste precious energy? Remain silent and 'observe' as Pure Soul unless it is necessary to speak. And prior to speaking, put your faith at your voice box so it can flow through you!

Verse #77

"There cannot be insistence with regards to 'real-relative' truth, where there is assertion, there is not 'real-relative' truth; 'Real-relative' truth prevails on it's own foundation."

ॐ

Reflective Flashes—

'My way or the high way', is the ultimate prescription for pain and dissention in the relative world. We must go with the flow. Our impact must be subtle, profound and without any doership. It must be based on the light that we create in the world with the rays of our Pure Soul. Therefore, any struggle or strife in the relative is deemed counterproductive for positive change. Yes, there is a need for change in this burning and caustic environment. It must be spiritually and subtly driven change that cannot be attributed to any one person or law! This is counterintuitive to everything we have learned in school! It really is against the grain as far as what we are taught to believe. We are taught to stand up for what is right and make a difference in the world. This is not untrue, however, how we go about it is the key. We must allow nature to execute our deepest wishes and desires for the world. The only change that we can truly make is in our self. The purer our relative self becomes, the bigger impact 'we' can have on positive change for the world. And that to is 'instrumental' impact!

Parenting is a great example for insistence. We might want our children to dress a certain way. We can enforce it like a dictator or with love and compassion convince our children to dress differently for the right reasons. Any form of dictatorship in the relative world is counterproductive and will not have positive results materially or spiritually. The key to unlocking our concerns for our children is love and compassion. We must see them as Pure Soul as well as our children in the relative world. In the relative world, our acceptance must be 100% unconditional. We must accept our children the way they are. Criticism is the worst form of child abuse. It forms scars that run very deep and will come back to bite us in the long run.

So, ultimately, prayer and staying seated in the Pure Soul is our prescription for living a life of reverence, joy and peace.

Verse #78

"Maintain only one main projection & association of 'I am Pure Soul'
absolutely, let all else flow with nature's natural currents."

ॐ

Reflective Flashes—

Analyzing life's events is too complicated! Unfortunately, we all do it. We
think that if we had done certain things differently, the outcome would
have been different. We are always looking for ways to solve the puzzle of
money making and life in general. It does not work that way! There is no
magic solution! We have to put out in order to receive back. The biggest
lesson learned with all the events is to remain true to oneself and one's
standards. Principle, morality and will power are definitely important to
keep dear to one's heart at all times.

There is no use in thinking about the past but our attachment and
detachment force us back! The traumatic events in our life are the one's
that keep haunting us. Sometimes these are actually perceived positive
events. There is intense attachment in these instances that keeps our
memory stuck there! On the other hand, some of us are stuck with
intensely traumatic and sad events that haunt us every day. It is difficult
to rise above them. The scars run deep so fight having to face them.
Anything bloody always turns stomachs!

The key to dealing effectively and proactively with cleaning all these
cobwebs from the past is to remain in the center and maintain the position
of observer at all times. 'See' the pain of our relative self and give a few pats
on the shoulder. Let the relative self know 'we' are with him/her. It sounds
crazy but it works! We must engage in some 'self' talk from the position
of being Pure Soul. It is actually speech powered by Pure Soul without the
indirect reflection of intellect. This 'self' talk is especially effective if done
with some heartfelt prayer to start.

Getting emotional will keep us from being centered. Allow all emotion
to be redirected for Pure Soul. This can still prove to be helpful. It is true
some personalities are just emotional by nature. It that emotion is fully
directed for the benefit of Pure Soul it is still acceptable. If that emotion
becomes 'relative'; this can create some pretty thick fog! It will result in
loss of clarity. Ultimately, will result in lack of spiritual progress. If we are
of an emotional energy engage in singing the beautiful songs written by
Kavi Raj or other uplifting music. They will serve to cleanse that emotion
of all its impurities.

Verse #79

"Know 'good' as 'good', know 'bad' as 'bad'; Stay completely free from attachment & detachment."

❧

Reflective Flashes—

Life is a dance. You must be vigilant and not miss a step or you will trip and fall. We are born with likes, dislikes, loves and hates. This is a fact of life. We must deal with this on a daily basis as it gushes through our karmic pipes. It's a good thing mother nature's pipes do not get rusty or clogged! We would be in serious trouble!

The key is to be aware and alert to our own hates and loves in this lifetime and through this educated observation those 'knots' of loves and hates our relative self will slowly move to the center. Many of our intense likes and dislikes stem from childhood memories and traumas. Ultimately, they are based on opinions we formed in the past. Most people fail to recognize this fact.

There is definitely a 'good' and a 'bad' code of behavior and ethics in the universe. Humans deep in their hearts know what is 'good' and what is 'bad'. The key is to be neutral and 'see' the good as 'good' and bad as 'bad' without having any opinion or attachment/detachment. We are now in the center as 'Pure Soul' after obtaining eternal truth from the Absolute Scientist so everything that occurs is now 'discharge'. It is water in the pipes that is draining after the valve has already been shut down. There is no new flow of water. This is the old water draining itself out. Just 'see and know' it.

The real freedom occurs when we stop having attachment and detachment for our relative self (File #1). This is the ultimate renunciation of the relative. When we cultivate the ability to just 'know and see' our relative self without any attachment and detachment everything else automatically falls into place. In order for this to happen, our loyalty and protection cannot be directed towards the relative self. We must view our relative self as a neighbor. That is the way it truly is! The reason we fall into the trap of 'good' and 'bad' and 'attachment and detachment' is because we are still loyal and protecting our relative self from defamation, disgrace and ridicule. Why? What is left to protect! There are so many things that are more important than the relative self! Let's get over ourselves already and focus on the 'real' well-being of the world! The view is so much better from the center anyways!

Verse #80

"Natural human tendencies & Pure Soul are separate & distinct, this is understood with divine separation knowledge of an Absolute Scientist; keep vigilantly watching the myriad natural tendencies."

༈

Reflective Flashes—

It seems that there should be a finite number of natural tendencies. However, there is infinite! Just equate it to the color wheel and all it's infinite possible shades. This is the vast variety of natural tendencies in human beings.

We were instruments to the design our own natural tendencies according to our own desires, wishes, opinions, likes and dislikes. The intense likes and dislikes from past karma are the things we either love or hate about ourselves! It's almost like being the person designing a house. We tell the architect, builders and masonry people what we want to see but the final result is not in our hands! It is in their hands. Similarly, we designed this mind, body and speech unknowingly with our opinions, hopes, desires, wishes and, of course, credit and debit karmas. The things we like are a result of our credit karma and the things we don't like are a result of our debit karma from the past.

From the core, we see our relative self and know every habit, tendency and fault of our neighbor, the relative self. The paradox of this knowledge is that by being non-doer we are moving mountains and instrumental to miracles occurring in the world. Doing nothing is the greatest achievement 'we' can accomplish! How ironic and paradoxical! In a world full of 'do this' and 'do that' at every turn; once planted firmly in Pure Soul, we are asked to be observer of the relative self and everything else in the universe. That is our mission and contract with the Absolute Scientist. We must learn to be true scientists through sincere and steadfast observation only. No judgments are to be passed. 'We' just 'see' and 'know' what our neighbor does 24/7. How incredible!

This is something that has never been heard of or told. It is 'real' in the realest sense. It is not for everyone. It is for those who truly taste the dryness of relative life. It is for those who do not find peace or joy in the relative life. It is for the old souls who need to move on from the cycle of birth and death.

Verse #81

"The senses that once roamed around everywhere outside will become totally steady in the brilliant soothing presence of the Pure Soul; That namely is known as retirement from the relative world."

❦

Reflective Flashes—

Many people are now searching for and engaging in meditation and yoga. Why? Because, we, as humans, have wished up a storm! There are so many distractions that it is difficult to stay focused. It is difficult for a married man or woman to keep his/her eyes on just one person. There are so many choices everywhere they go! People are marrying once, twice, thrice and in even more in some cases! The baby boomers are denying they are almost seniors! They think they will live forever. This crazy mentality is giving rise to chaos. WE as a human race created this craziness. We will be affected by proportionate to what we contributed to the creation of this craziness. The sad thing is that the distractions that were wished-up are all focused on the pleasure of the five senses. This creates a dilemma for the family structure that is so sadly lacking in the Western world. Families are being ripped apart and children are growing up with huge scars that will show their ramifications in the future. This is not healthy and will never be healthy. Now that things have come to a pinnacle, there is the search for peace and grounding through Eastern practices such as meditation and yoga. This is helpful!

Many are planning for retirement as early as their 20s, 30s and naturally in their 40s and 50s. What is the meaning of 'retirement'? Whether we retire or not from our occupations, there is always social obligations, financial obligations and physical obligations to take care of. That is not retirement! After the kids are gone, there are grandchildren to think about and enjoy. It does not end!

Renouncing the worldly life is not 'retirement'. Giving up work and family obligations is not retirement. Running from the people who are connected to you is not retirement. Doing only things that you love is not retirement. True 'retirement' from the relative world is to be in the center as Pure Soul; steadfast, strong and ready to 'see and know' whatever may be in store in the karmic pipeline for this lifetime. THAT is the meaning of 'true' retirement!

Verse #82

" 'Who Am I?' if that is known, there is nothing more left to be known; without that knowledge, all is completely useless and wasted."

⤶

Reflective Flashes—

Since infinite lives we have been searching for pleasure, happiness, joy or whatever we want to call it. Because of this thirst for happiness, we have bound countless karma resulting in infinite cycles of birth-and-death. It has been a long and frustrating journey. For infinite lives, our relative self has morphed continuously to different life forms and different human forms. If we have been fortunate enough to meet the Absolute Scientist and obtain knowledge of 'Who Am I' from Him, this human life has been the most fruitful and should be revered highly. This human body and life has become a temple as a result of getting the golden pedestal of Pure Soul through this embodiment. This does not mean we are to pamper and spoil this human temple! We just need to recognize that this neighbor is our best friend and vice versa! We found our permanent home through this vessel. How valuable it is even though it will perish with unite with the ashes of the earth one day! The existence through which an Absolute Scientist is met is priceless!

Permanent happiness or joy is not to be found in any place. Many of us have searched high, low, in the heavens and in hell looking for permanent happiness for infinite lives. We have greatly complicated our lives through wanting more and better thus become instrumental in the chaotic state that we live our lives. Simple is better and less is truly more. We have forgotten how to enjoy the simple joys of living. Our children are drinking milk of cows treated with growth hormones. We are drinking milk of cows treated with growth hormones. What does this do to us as a society? It makes us unnatural. The girls and boys are growing up too quickly. The innocence of youth is lost at ungodly ages. Is this healthy? We, as the human race, have asked nature for this. Nature is neutral and must deliver what we ask for! How ignorant are we and were we to ask for this nuttiness?

If an Absolute Scientist has given the golden threshold of Pure Soul, do not allow this priceless gift to go to waste. Stay within those five divine dictates and be 'instrumental' in the realigning of the human race. The God within each and every living being knows we need the help! Let's pay infinite 'kudos' and 'gratitude' to the Absolute Scientist for all His grace and compassion.

Verse #83

"The worship that occurs with the understanding of the 'Gyani Purush' or Absolute Scientist as an embodiment of Pure Soul; that worship is of the highest form oriented towards the attainment of absolute 'Pure Soul'."

ॐ

Reflective Flashes—

We cannot fool anyone in this life anymore! Judgment day has come. Everything is going back to being transparent. It is not possible to fool anyone anymore! We cannot even fool ourselves! Things are becoming crystal clear. This is happening because of the presence of the Absolute Scientist on this earth. It is not fathomable with the human eyes to see the intricate workings of His presence as He lives on this earth. He can accomplish thousands of things in one breath! We cannot even begin to imagine the power of an Absolute Scientist. We will just live to see the results.

The purity of our understanding will determine the purity of our worship. The Absolute Scientist cannot be understood through the intellect. He is always in an omniscient state of being. He is always totally present. He lives from nano-second to nano-second. His grace and compassion know NO bounds. He will bless His worst enemy. He will shower one who scorns Him openly with blessings. His pure love has no boundaries. He lives to liberate others. His only intention 24/7 is to help others to attain permanent peace, joy and love. He realizes that people have forgotten how to live. He is here to mend hearts, weld minds and bring peace and progress to the world as well as grant knowledge of the Pure Soul. Pure love is more vast than the deepest and widest oceans. It is limitless. It can permeate even the most blackened heart within minutes. Most black hearts became that way due to lack of pure love! He has the command of all the demi-gods and demi-goddesses. His power is not by force! They are there to grant anything that He asks. They want to protect and uphold Him because of His purity. He often will ask the demi-gods and demi-goddesses to help His followers with worldly problems in certain situations. He is neutral in every sense of the word. He is completely free from attachment. This means He does not even own a shred of detachment towards any living being or thing in this universe. He is a royal king in His own right that has never and will never be a beggar for relative anything!

Verse #84

"What is truly yours can never be lost, what does not belong to you will not stay around; that is the exact law of nature."

ॐ

Reflective Flashes—

This is true in the relative world as well as the 'real' world. It is a lot like the parent who loves their child so dearly they are willing to let that child go! If the child comes back, he/she was truly theirs to begin with! First, we must let go of all. What remains with us is ours. After knowledge of Pure Soul, we are rich beyond belief. There is no sense of dissatisfaction or thirst left within us. We are only ready to accept that which is ours. Therefore, we must let go! We must accept and settle for the ways of the world without a fight. With pure and sound understanding, we must let go. Whatever is left was ours to begin with! One day this human body will unite with the earth. What else, then, can be truly 'ours'? Treat all things and people with respect and love, but be willing to let go without a shred of regret or ill feeling at any time. This is the code of conduct of a true warrior of the Pure Soul.

There are many people who will engage in pre-nuptial agreements. Why? If people are willing to make the sacrifice and commitment of marriage to another living being, why the restrictions, fear and negative slant from the outset? It is a holy matrimony. In Indian scriptures it is written that marriage is a spiritual union of two living beings for the purpose of attaining liberation. It is a union between two groups of people. The purpose is to elevate both groups as a result of the union. Indian people are keeping the in-laws out of their homes and are not honoring the ways of our ancestors. This is a direct insult to their own heritage. We were taught to honor and respect our elders no matter what the situation. That tradition is rotting away. Honor, respect, dignity and pride are being sold-out for pleasure seeking of the five senses. Luckily, many of the elders have understood the new ways and have let go.

For those who have not, we hear about early deaths from heart attacks and cancer. This poor generation has learned this lesson in a bitter and scathing manner. The lesson being that in the relative world all relationships and things are temporary. Anything can happen at any time! Be true to the permanent Pure Soul of every living being at every turn in life. That choice will never steer us in the wrong direction. Value what is worth being valued and revered.

Verse #85

"Whatever actions are taken, the counter-reactions will ultimately penalize; None other can ever come to punish."

༈

Reflective Flashes—

The skeletons in the closet are our own creations from the past. They will show their repercussions regardless of our memory of them. Someone who seemingly has cleaned-up their act will suddenly start having bad luck at every turn. Everyone feels bad and wonders why nature is punishing him/her after he/she has changed his ways! Well, what about all the garbage he/she gathered along the way? It has to be cleared out! Similarly, we have come with some trash and some salvageable things that must be cleared-out regardless of value.

The things we suffer in innocence were done unknowingly. The things we suffer with understanding were done knowingly or on purpose. A child who suffers from sexual abuse does not understand the horrible affliction that is being afflicted. The repercussions stay with that child for a lifetime, however, the actual suffering is in an innocent state of being. The crime, therefore, was done in ignorance. Fortunately, most children of abuse that realize and face up to their abuse are able to deal with it once they understand the reasons for their anguish. So, with knowledge, they are able to overcome their pain. The man who knowingly cheated on his wife will suffer the consequences knowingly. The suffering is more acute in proportion to the level of understanding of the crime. If something is done on purpose and with an evil intention, the repercussions are quite severe in the future.

Crimes that involve other living beings become quite complicated as revenge and hatred come into play. Nature has the daunting task of playing-out the karma according to the good deeds, bad deeds and intentions of the parties involved. We have really managed to make mother nature work way too hard in this wacky world! Depending on the level of intensity of the relationship, it can be the same souls or in many instances different souls that come together to settle the accounts.

There are also the fruits of the good deeds that must be experienced as well. The positive account balances must be spent in order to bring the balance to zero! It is important to remain vigilant so as not to become immersed and get trapped in these 'sweet' times. Circumstances are temporary regardless!

Verse #86

"When one becomes the bearer & owner of the fruits of past karma, new seeds of karma are planted; as knower-perceiver only there is perfect & complete purging of karma."

༄

Reflective Flashes—

Purging of karma sounds so great! It is relieving and exhilarating to think that the accounts are being cleared and the quest for true freedom is being accomplished. It is so much easier said than done. It is kind of like cleaning a home. It is easy to stuff things in closets, dressers and cupboards. However, the true cleaning of a home requires much time, energy and attention to detail. We must be positive that our hearts, minds and intentions are pure in every situation that we encounter in our lives. This is what true purging requires! If we do not want to bind additional karma for the next life we must be transparent and no agendas can be left in the closet! Our lives must be like living in a fish bowl where there is no place to hide with any hidden agendas. This is for our benefit, not the benefit of others. We must understand this fully! We are the ones who want eternal bliss and freedom; not the world. It behooves us to make our goal happen! We have been given all the tools we need by the Absolute Scientist so let's not disgrace Him in all His infinite grace.

Our greatest accomplishment after attaining knowledge from the Absolute Scientist is renouncing ownership of this mind, body and speech. We must hold our 'neighbor' accountable in every way, however, 'we' must always remain 100% neutral towards our 'neighbor'. The trials and tribulations that our relative self faces are the result of false projections. The fun and games that the relative self faces are also the result of false projections. It is all 'relative'. It is all discharge regardless of flavor. Some circumstances are a dull gray, some a bright hot pink, some a tantalizing yellow and the spectrum is infinite.

Our goal is perfection in purging the karma. How can we bring the balances to zero? It is our duty to guide our relative self towards us and away from the ways of the relative world. Gently chastise, gently pamper and gently turn the 'neighbor' around to the eternal. It is in the best interest of the universe!

Verse #87

"The world goes on instinctively & without fail with its in-built natural laws, live compliantly & cooperatively according to the way of the world; without any waves of friction, all flows smoothly."

⤳

Reflective Flashes—

People like to say, 'Go with the flow.' This is such a wise statement! There is no point in creating waves in a world that is already burning intensely with the flames of pain, anger, hatred, revenge and greed. It would be like adding fuel to a fire that is already burning out-of-control.

Who are we to attempt to correct the world? Only prayer has the power to move mountains and change the world. That is the one power we do have! The power of prayer is beyond the reach of scientists! It is a vehicle to transport the powers of the Pure Soul into the relative world! If we think deeply about this statement, it is quite profound!

The material world has far out run the spiritual world in this age. When this occurs, the tremendous power of the Pure Soul is nowhere to be found! Everything is about the external world that is experienced through the five senses. How can it be done faster, cheaper and with ease? We have email that allows us to communicate a letter or statement within a matter of minutes thousands of miles across the world. We were amazed with the power of the telephone. That gave birth to the thoughts of having the ability to communicate with words and pictures. Thus, the internet, email and digital photos! Technology will continue to evolve. The sad thing is the human spirit and the power of character has been lost in this quest for sleeker, faster, and easier! Who will teach our children to be responsible human beings? Who will teach them about compassion, love and the important lessons of life? If we have none of the above, how can we pass them along to our children? If we put our value on the real amidst this onslaught of material focus, there is hope!

We can only lead by example. Children learn what they live, smell, breathe and hear on a daily basis.

So, stay seated on the royal throne of radiant Pure Soul and live a life of purpose and purity. The relative self is a temporary shell. It is our temple until it pops and unites with mother earth one day. Allow the Pure Soul to shine brightly through this temple no matter how broken, faulty or pathetic it may be!

Verse #88

"Happy & sad times are of a departing transitory nature, they come & go;
they are within the laws of the pre-recorded impartial cosmic computer
software energy."

௸

Reflective Flashes—

There is no power greater than that of Mother Nature! Every situation
that arises, we have a choice to clear the account or bind new karma. We
must be vigilant and take the every possible step we are able in the relative
to ensure we have fulfilled our duty. Once that has been done, only then we
are to leave the rest to the impartial cosmic energy to settle the accounts.
Life is almost like a business. There is a give and take that occurs.
There are vendors, customers, suppliers, regulatory agencies, insurance
companies, banks, marketing, sales, technology and other functions to
deal with. It is quite a puzzle running a business! It is important to have a
business plan!
Our plan for life is to clear the accounts. Let's keep it simple! Whatever
went into the cosmic computer is what will come out. Life is what it is.
The intentions and opinions that were fed into the cosmic computer must
be expressed! It is inevitable. The biggest gift is to be able to let go of all
those situations and the impact that they had on us. All situations leave
their mark on us in some way or another. The key is to 'see'. See what the
reactions are, see what the words are, and see how the ego, mind, intellect
and heart react in all situations.
This does not mean we are to become robots or devoid of emotion. The
emotion can be channeled in the direction of Pure Soul. The sad truth
is that we have no power right now! The only power we have as human
beings is the power to be positive, suck-it-up and, if we know our Pure Soul,
remain completely separate from the 'happenings'.
Joy is an emotion that can only be experienced through the medium of the
heart. It is not tainted by anything impure. Joy is the thrill of being alive.
The relative self can only experience joy if there is purity of the heart.
Happy and sad are relative and transitory conditions. We must 'see' the
happiness and the sadness that is experienced by our best friend, our
neighbor, our relative self. 'We', as Pure Soul, must have compassion for
the results of ignorance, pain, sorrow and darkness that our neighbor
endures.

Verse #89

"Sacred scriptures are known as a path, absolute peace, enlightenment
& satisfaction cannot be found there; Absolute peace, enlightenment &
satisfaction can only be found in the heart of a 'Gyani'."

જ

Reflective Flashes–

A 'Gyani' is just another name for an Absolute Scientist. Book knowledge
is just that: Book knowledge. The true meaning of 'reading' any book is
to take away at least 2 things that can be tested, researched or immediately
utilized in order to enrich our lives and elevate our state of being. This
is the purpose of scriptures: To give direction and ideas for progress.
We have roamed for infinite lives. We need a 'real' solution. We need
something that will never allow us to be thirsty or 'empty' inside ever again.
Most people today have holes in their hearts (figuratively speaking). Just as
a stone gets smooth as it gets tossed from here to there over the years, the
heart gets round holes from the wear and tear of infinite lives. These holes
represent emptiness. The more times we get burned, the emptier we feel.
The only permanent medicine for this is knowledge and experience of Pure
Soul. This knowledge and experience can only be obtained from a 'Gyani'.
What an incredible achievement it is to be able to say, 'I am totally
satisfied. I have no wishes or wants. No feelings of longing for anything.'
Basically, most humans are beggars. People are beggars in the sense that
they are 'begging' for something temporary in this world to please the
five senses or satisfy the ego. Most people pray for things, for children,
for health, for wealth or for their loved ones. Who prays for liberation?
Who really wants to be free? There are not too many people who pray for
freedom. It takes quite an old soul to be searching for permanent joy and
peace. It is not any easy road to take. It takes courage and persistence to
be steadfast in the conviction for liberation. Since most of the world is
not in that quest, it will actually be like swimming against the tide! Many
people will think that we have lost our minds! Others will think we are
terribly boring! That is okay. What is our goal? It is to clear the accounts!
Most people let 'crazy' or 'boring' people go! They write them off. If 'we'
are to reach our goal, the safest haven is the heart of the Absolute Scientist.
He will not let us down. We must be strong in our conviction and practice
the science according to His direction. The essence of all scriptures is
contained in His five divine dictates.

Verse #90

"Showering with flowers & the throwing of stones are both just worldly 'relative' happenings; what was dished-out must now be received, it's a boomerang effect."

ॐ

Reflective Flashes—

Those who insult, reject, exile, belittle, ridicule and betray are all 'angels in disguise'. They are the ones who are instruments to removing the 'sweet juice' from our ego. Our ego will not go down easily. It has had a reign for infinite lives. Will it go down peacefully? No way! See not those who have shunned, betrayed and put daggers in your heart as enemies. They are mere instruments to our elevation. We must become extremely light and humble to get the 'exact' essence of this science. Wash the feet of those 'angels in disguise' daily for they are innocent instruments on the path to liberation. This is the only way to guard against building revengeful karma. Do it daily if not hourly! If the memory of these innocent instruments haunts our being, then keep washing those feet until it fades away forever. They are in our lives due to our bad deeds from previous lives. If we have many, then we should know what kind of crooked understanding we had in our past lives! BEWARE! Stay firmly seated on the golden threshold of Pure Soul and allow the events to unfold. If it helps, pick out at least 2 appealing qualities of those people and focus on those, but, do NOT build revengeful intentions. They are innocent instruments.

On the other hand, beware of those who shower with flowers. They are innocent instruments as well. However, they are in our lives due to our good deeds. It is important to be extra vigilant with these instruments since we lose ourselves in the 'sweetness' of these relationships. That means we forget our identity as 'Pure Soul' and become immersed in the 'sweetness' of the relationship. BEWARE! This relative life is all 'dramatic' only. We are not to get blinded by the false illusions of worldly love, lust, infatuation, friendship, and support. They are all 'business' transactions. We are simply squaring the accounts. Sometimes it is more enjoyable to square certain accounts than others. That is fine. We must not forget that it is temporary and relative after all. The royal throne of Pure Soul is not worth leaving even for one second! If we practice this sincerely, our compassion for others will start overflowing.

Verse #91

"Without the worldly relative nothing is received, what was wound now unwinds; without having given, it absolutely cannot be received."

∿

Reflective Flashes—

Longing and emptiness in the heart are very sad to experience. What we had given in the past lives is all that can be received. If we only put 60 cents in the soda machine, how can we get two sodas? If we only deposit $500 dollars in the bank and we write a check for $1000, what happens? We get into trouble! We get charged fees and the check bounces. How fun is that? Our opinions from the past are what are being manifested in this lifetime. It cannot be changed. It must be seen. The film is playing already. If we do not like it, we do not have the luxury to walk out of the theatre. We are tied at the hip to our neighbor, our best friend and ultimately the reason for us finding our Pure Soul. At least give that much credit to this relative self. The give and take in the relative life is all a result of past karmic accounts. There is nothing more to it! It sounds so simple yet it becomes so complex due to ignorance or lack of commitment to Pure Soul. Once we have filled our hearts with a conviction for liberation, there should be NO longing for ANY worldly desires. Nothing needs to be renounced... it is the longing that should disappear. If we get something, we are fine with it and if we do not get something we should be fine with it. That is the litmus test for how close or far we are from the center.

This life is a test whether we have knowledge of Pure Soul or not. Life is far from rosy these days. Most people feel lucky to make it through each day without falling into an abyss of darkness and despair. The world truly is in a bad state.

We cannot compare our lives to any else's. Our life is our own creation. Our own intentions, deeds (both good and bad), hopes, dreams, opinions and convictions bring our life to materialization. We had input our own material, spiritual, personal, and professional results. The impartial cosmic computer does the coding of our data. Imagine what a tremendous job this poor overworked computer has! We are sapping nature in all our greed and zest for the relative life. We want it all! Mother nature does not complain! We, in all our imperfection of input, complain when we see the results!

Verse #92

"If fires are set, the heat will have to be experienced, without friction no one will disturb; if you are straightforward, the world will be straightforward."

ॐ

Reflective Flashes—

There is so much to be experienced outside of the five senses! The problem is that there is a constant search to stimulate and entertain the five senses. What about the incredible power and joy of experiencing Pure Soul? That has never been known. It has been tasted but not known. People do not know the incredible depth of experience of the Pure Soul. It is beyond words. It is deep and enthralling. It is like being immersed in an ocean of love, peace, joy and knowledge without any of the risks of truly being in an ocean!

In order to achieve this state, the work is all-internal. The 'real' effort lies within. From the outside, it may appear that people with 'real' knowledge from the Absolute Scientist are complacent and wimpy (without a backbone). Actually, it is the opposite. There is a tremendous energy and power that emanates from being in the center. That energy is natural and cannot be explained through the intellect.

It behooves those of us who do have knowledge from the Absolute Scientist to live a life free from any friction. It is not in our hands, however, it should most definitely be a strong conviction. This is the way to project the most light from knowing Pure Soul. The light will get brighter and wider as the level of non-violence rises to the point of being negligible through complete non-doership and understanding.

What brings people together? Karma. There is no other more exact answer. There cannot be an exchange of words, meeting of the minds, or locking of eyes without some karmic connection. If our intention and conviction is pure and clear now, it will surpass the garbage from the past. The effect of the past karma on others will be significantly lightened if our conviction today is to clear the accounts. Even if there is ugly and dark history attached to a karmic link, it will not be as pronounced and lingering as it otherwise would be without the light of the Pure Soul. In other words, with the conviction for Pure Soul, all karma gets lightened ten to thousand fold.

Each morning the intense and steadfast conviction must be reinforced that it is our intention to have clash, conflict or friction with any living being. Our goal is to amicably clear the accounts without creating any fires.

Verse #93

"You are bound by your mistakes; you're grip keeps you inside your own self-made trap; Release that grip then freedom from bondage is yours."

ॐ

Reflective Flashes—

Why do people worry so much about what other people think? Most of the time, people are so concerned about themselves they really do not even take the time to really evaluate another person. It is important to come to grips with our own identity. Take 100% responsibility for our own karma, our own life, our own everything and resolve to clear the mess that has been created. There is no need to worry about what others think.

Once we take ownership of our own mistakes, we are free from them. It is paradoxical, however, it is a fact. It is only possible to see our own faults if we are separate. This means once we have been blessed with the realization of the Pure Soul from the Absolute Scientist, this process of seeing the faults of our 'neighbor, our best friend, our relative self' can begin. The biggest blunder that we must let go of is 'I am this person'. That is the first gargantuan wrong belief.

It is important to take care of our best friend as a true best friend really would care for and guide a best friend. The grip that we need to let go of is the need and desire to try and control the relative. The relative life is pure discharge. It is not to be messed with. It is not okay to give others a hard time or make waves in the relative. Our job, as Pure Soul, is to guide, support and discipline the relative self. The relative self is now our neighbor. 'We' as Pure Soul do not identify with the faults of the relative self. We 'know and see' them. We gently cajole our neighbor to do confession, repentance and confirmation when our neighbor makes a mistake.

'We' as Pure Soul are free! The relative self must do the work. It is the relative self that is bound! However, without the clearance of the accounts, 'we' cannot be permanently free. So, it is in our best interest to ensure the relative self is comfortable, focused and alert. We need our neighbor on our side! If we need to give our neighbor a pat on the back once in a while, what is the harm in doing it? It is, after all, in our best interest.

For those without knowledge of Pure Soul, it is still beneficial to understand this concept to help one live a life of self-purification.

Verse #94

*"If permanent association with Pure Soul is attained, everything rolls
along smoothly without any hitches; Obstacles will themselves move aside."*

ॐ

Reflective Flashes—

How to achieve this permanent association? The irony is that we are
permanent by our very own nature; however, have to reacquaint ourselves
with our own Self due to our grave wrong beliefs of infinite lives. Anything
related to time is temporary! Time is limitless; yet, anything connected to
time is temporary. The Pure Soul is infinite, pure, and always has been and
always will be. Therefore, time and Pure Soul have a couple of qualities in
common. Time is permanent, constant and limitless and so is Pure Soul. If
we start living our lives as Pure Soul and not as the relative self, we become
permanent and timeless. This concept is a little subtle and can be difficult
to grasp without a direct experience of Pure Soul.

Obstacles in the relative life are due to our bad deeds, opinions and
dislikes of the past. If we caused someone an obstacle to eating, we will
have obstacles for eating in our life. If we caused an obstacle to someone
studying, we could have obstacles to achieving our educational goals. If we
kept someone from having a relationship with someone they love, then we
will have obstacles in having the relationships we would like to have with
our loved ones. Whenever we encounter an obstacle in our lives, we must
realize we must have been an obstacle, caused an obstacle or supported
someone obstructing another living being in our past lives. Nothing
happens without a reason.

When 'we' begin to see the faults of our own relative self, then the
transformation begins. Once there is accountability, confession,
repentance, and confirmation for the mistakes and blunders, the obstacles
start moving quite rapidly. For some, there are more obstacles and for
others there are fewer obstacles. The key is to be focused in the center and
allow all the garbage to be cleared-out. This mind, body and speech will
ultimately unite with the earth where it came from. What about us? What
are 'we' left with? This is where the true value of Pure Soul can be realized.
Most people do not think deeply about these concepts, however, there is
no guarantee of long lives for anyone. It is never too early to start thinking
about our spiritual goals.

There is no greater power than to see the Pure Soul of every living being.

Verse #95

"Whatever comes is by natural account balance, one who understands this puts it in the ledger whether it be profit or loss; whatever occurs is complete & natural justice."

✦

Reflective Flashes—

This can be a bitter and sad truth and it can be a sweet and sour truth! It is what it is. No one can dispute this truth. Yes, through the windows of intellect, arguments can be made. Yes, through the attitude of 'Who cares' that is so prevalent today, it can be defied. However, life is what it is. No one can change that. What occurs is complete and natural justice no matter how we may try to deny it!

We are taught to fight back and not be spineless in our lives. This is not untrue, however, it is directed towards our ethics and morals. Our spine needs to be made of steel with regards to our ethics and morals. Unfortunately, those have been so underrated today to the point of being non-existent! Furthermore, have those values and ethics been instilled in our lives by our elders? This is an age of weak people. Most people have little will power. They are unable to resist the temptations of the five senses. They are easily swayed by the actions of others. People are like sheep following others. Human life is far too valuable to be wasted on following others around like sheep!

Today is a result. Tomorrow is a result. Everyday of our lives is a result. Why fight it? Accept the results of our own karma. It is our best friend who is getting their results. If our best friend feels bad about the results, 'we' can console him/her. Why fret? Why worry? Make the best of the situation. Our biggest concern is that our intentions are in the right place. The intent is to clear the accounts no matter what price we must pay emotionally, mentally or physically. That is all temporary. What counts is protecting the territory of the 'real' Pure Soul. The goal is to have the Pure Soul win. For infinite lives, the relative self has had its glory and it's pride. It is time for the Pure Soul to have a chance at permanent reign.

In the relative, everything is relative. There cannot be any laws or regulations for we crazy humans formulated them in the past. Mother nature is now just delivering the packages as they arrive through the funnel.

Verse #96

"This is all about debit & credit entries, the account self-balances
accordingly; It is the law of the pre-recorded impartial cosmic computer
software energy called 'vyavasthit shakti'."

༄

Reflective Flashes—

This whole concept can be a little difficult to digest as 'doership' has
haunted us for infinite lives. When we move our little hands and legs, when
we think something that is benevolent and kind, we think 'we' are the doer.
What about when we get awful thoughts. Are we the doer then? What
about when we hurt others through our mind, body and speech, then are
we still doer? If we get highly educated and get a high paying position at a
Fortune 100 Company, we pride ourselves. What if we get laid off the next
day? Are we to take credit for that as well? We have high hopes and great
intentions for our children. What if they tragically get killed in an auto
accident? Are we to take the blame for that? Are we doers?

Human nature is such that it likes to take credit for the good stuff and
push off the responsibility for the bad stuff on God, circumstances, luck
or even other people! The bottom line is that we came with a certain
amount of credit balance and a certain amount of debit balance. They will
undoubtedly be exhausted. It does not really work like a general ledger in
accounting because the debit and credit entries do not necessarily impact
one another. There could be a credit balance when it comes to family and
friends. There could be a debit balance when it comes to relations with
business associates. It all depends on how the intentions and opinions
were fed into the cosmic computer in the past. The impartial cosmic
computer allocates according to intensity of intention and opinion. Our
deepest passions are where it allocates our credit balances first. Then, as
the intensity of the passion decreases, that particular aspect is allocated
according to what is left. For example if someone feels it is really important
to have a great mother and it does not really matter what the wife is like,
that is where the credit and debit balances will get applied respectively.
Essentially, what we get that we like is where our credit balance was applied
and what we do not like is a result of our debit balance from our past lives.
This is not from this life's dealings, doings or deeds.

Verse #97

" 'What's happened & occurred' why did it happen? Don't speculate & question; 'What's happened & occurred' is in perfect and exact natural order."

⤚

Reflective Flashes—

Why? Why? Why? We have all asked ourselves these questions with regards to many of life's events, tragedies and disappointments. This is healthy in one sense because it helps us develop the passion to *know*. However, it can become a disease if we do not keep a limit to our inquisitiveness. The healthiest way to want to know is through the heart, not the intellect! If we question and look for answers through the intellect, we will get reflected and shadowed answers. We need 'real' answers! That can only be found through the heart and from heartfelt prayer to an Absolute Scientist. The answers are all there; our intentions and prayers must be PURE to achieve 'real' results. The irony of it all is that when we let go of our demand for answers and live as Pure Soul, the answers automatically start pouring in without any invitation at all!

When everything starts to go wrong, we wonder why? Why me? What did I do? This is natural! However, we do not know what is in the pipeline. We can project positive outcomes for everything. We can keep a positive attitude, however, only that which is in the pipeline can come through! When things go sour it is our lack of credit balance. We did not bring enough of the credit balance with us to have things go our way in the relative! It truly was our own projection. We do not realize this now, however, that is exactly the way it is. The good news is that for every relative occurrence there is always a positive and negative side. The relative is always like a chemical reaction. There are two equal and opposite sides to it! We must learn to see the positive when 'horrible' and 'saddening' events occur. Furthermore, when things seem really sweet and likeable, we need to counterbalance by recognizing the down side. In other words, we must always remain normal. In the face of adversity and rejection, we must remain calm and normal. In the face of love and acceptance, we must remain calm and normal. These are the true tests of our neutrality. As Pure Soul, we are in the center; completely untouched and separate from the 'relative' happenings. Our neighbor does the relative drama and even gets saddened or elated, 'we' must be there to either 'pick-up' or 'bring down' our best friend at those times. How incredible is this science!?

Verse #98

"The causes that were previously endorsed, manifest as physical circumstances (results); there can never be a change in the result outside of the causes which were planted."

༄

Reflective Flashes—

Whether we want to face this grim fact or not, we created this result. Whether we like it or not, we must deal with it. This is our own result. Let's not cry over spilled milk! It was spilled in the last life. We are cleaning-up the mess in this one! Let's do it with dignity and self-respect no matter how difficult it may seem to be! Grin and bear it, suck-it-up, whatever we want to call it, we must move forward with dignity and equanimity. We cannot throw up our hands and say 'I give up'. That will not work. We must work through the trials and tribulations to the best of our abilities in the relative and remain knower-perceiver in the real. Depression is not an option. It is an easy trap to fall into, however, for those with knowledge and experience of Pure Soul, it is off limits! We cannot use that excuse!!! There are pills to treat the chemical imbalances that cause depression that millions of people are consuming and thus making the pharmaceutical companies rich. Our 'pill' is Pure Soul. 'We' can never allow our best friend and neighbor to become depressed for more than 5 minutes! It is our job to keep our best friend on an even keel! The things that constantly bite us are the places where we held intense attachment or hatred. Whether it is towards a person, place or thing, it will keep biting our being until we flush out the biases we hold towards that person, place or thing. Sometimes that person can be our relative self's attitude towards our relative self. This is self-inflicted hatred or excessive attachment towards oneself. Our biggest file is our file #1! The next 'sticky' file is #2. We get emotions of intense attachment, detachment, jealousy, resentment, guilt, pity and a whole gamut of human emotions that are quite intense. How do deal with these? Talk to the neighbor! Talk to the best friend! Sit in front of the mirror and reason out the irrational thoughts and emotions. It sounds ludicrous but it is the only way!

Verse #99

"One 'relative' and another 'real', decipher the world with these two viewpoints; the pre-recorded impartial cosmic computer software energy runs each living being's circumstances."

⌘

Reflective Flashes—

When it seems like the whole world is out to get you and you only, it is so wonderful to have the golden threshold of Pure Soul as a haven. It is easy to feel vulnerable and hurt when the going gets tough in the relative. It is so beautiful and we are so fortunate to have the two viewpoints to live by. The key is to remember that when things so sour in the relative, we get that much stronger in the real! It is a law of nature! The scales will always balance themselves according to our settings!

When the going gets tough in the relative, take the opportunity to make progress in the real. No moment in this human life is worth wasting! Let's be focused and learn how to manage our energies no matter what is occurring in the relative life. Maximizing return on investment in our human life form is the key to a successful life both materially and spiritually!

It is a fact that the pre-recorded impartial cosmic computer software energy runs each and every living being's circumstances. This is indisputable. We are, with or without knowledge of Pure Soul, at the mercy of other forces and energies. People believe through superstition and misdirected faith that they have the power to do and change circumstances.

Yes, we can change our attitude. That is a wonderful and miraculous power. That and the power to wish, intend, pray and project are also part of our powers. We are not powerless. We have been sadly ignorant for infinite lives of our true powers. A single word spoken from the heart with love and humility can mend a broken heart. This is the power we possess as human beings. The power of projecting pure love to even our worst enemies is true power. This can only be achieved by the fewest of the few and the luckiest of the lucky.

We have no need for sunglasses or eyeglasses any more. We have our perfect vision granted by the Absolute Scientist. This helps us to see things just exactly as they are both in the relative and the real.

Verse #100

"Our relations of the past, regulate them with neutral intentions; from now forward, uphold, protect & identify with the Pure Soul."

జ

Reflective Flashes—

The accounts are being squared no matter how the justice may appear to be flawed. This is a cold hard fact we have discussed throughout this little book. Let's not get overly analytical. It does not help! We must allow the knowledge to work. We must ask our 'intellect' to sit aside as this is knowledge of the heart and soul at work. It is a permanent solution. It is not like washing with soap that will leave its residue to be removed later on. This is IT. We must be alert, vigilant and brave on the path of liberation. This is truly not even a path. It is a fact. The science of absolutism is reality. It is live. There is no path or dress rehearsal. Every circumstance is an opportunity to become that much closer to being absolute in every sense once the Pure Soul has been realized.

We have roamed for infinite lives without giving up on the relative! Why give up now? This is one of the final laps in the marathon of infinite lives. We must not get caught up in wanting absolute perfection in the relative. We strive to our utmost efforts to live a clash free and harmonious existence. When conflicts do arise, we must remain humble and give whatever needs to be given in order to settle the account. If the ego of that person needs to be fed, let it be. If we must listen quietly to bitter and scathing words, let it be. If we must admit our wrong, let it be. If we must bow our heads in defeat, let it be. If we must put on a show, let it be. If we must shed tears to show remorse, let it be. WHATEVER it takes, our goal is to settle the account so there is no claim from the other side!

Our bias is definitely towards the Pure Soul in any situation, not our relative self. People may even think we have gone crazy. That is okay. We must many times lose to win in the relative. We are not living this life for fame, money, respect or accolades. We are here to square the accounts. Everything else that is received is a by-product whether sweet, sour, bitter or tasteless. It is all discharge. Let's not live our lives with any sort of remorse or regret. We have IT. We have our Pure Soul. The Absolute Scientist has put us in the center. There is nothing more left to discover! We have not a clue how truly blessed and fortunate we are!

Verse #101

"Relatives, loved ones and all kin far and near, they are all signed sealed contracted relationships from the past; the stipulations or wagers have been made to attain freedom for and from all."

❧

Reflective Flashes—

We have embarked upon a mission for total and absolute freedom. That means we want to permanently unite with God. God is our own Pure Soul. It makes perfect sense. The relationships we have forged for infinite lives are numerous and complex. It is no cakewalk just 'letting go' of it all. This must be done with pure and complete understanding of the Science of Absolutism. We are letting go of the relative and temporary, yet, embracing the 'real'. There is no loss involved here! However, due to infinite lives of conditioning, our relative self will try to convince us that we are cheating others and ourselves out of the true joys of living. This is not the case! That evil intellect will raise its ugly head if we do not keep it in check. There is nothing false or pretentious in our living either. We are actually embracing life with all its true joys. There is no room for pretending or sublimation in the Science of Absolutism. The truth is that our vision, which was faulty, is now correct. We know relative for what it is and we know real for what it is. Our knowledge and experience of the relative is of infinite lives. We have just been officially acquainted with the 'real' recently. There is more effort in knowing, experiencing and maximizing the 'real' as it is something new to us.

The bets are on! There is no turning back. If we do, it will be so painful and dry that we will not be able to bear it! It is like the person who lives in a lush tropical paradise and is thrown into an arid and dry desert without any food or water. We cannot turn our backs on Pure Soul! It is our very identity. We will literally lose our minds if we try to go back to ignorance. Fear of the unknown causes roadblocks. We must not live in fear. We are empowered and we are meant to make a difference in our world with this priceless gift we have obtained from the Absolute Scientist.

When in doubt, just listen to your heart. Listen intently without any outer noise. Your heart will tell you the value of Pure Soul.

Verse #102

"The world is always on fire, its very nature is to burn; the knower-perceiver-seer will never get burnt."

ↄ♠ↄ

Reflective Flashes—

We cannot forget the nature of water is to run downward. Also, it is the nature of gravity to pull things down. These are natural forces. Similarly, the world's nature is to be chaotic. There cannot be fire without friction. There is tremendous friction in our world. The fires are innumerable at every turn. The term 'fire' is a metaphor for conflict. The nature of this world is towards conflict. There is little harmony to be found. When there is harmony, it does not last very long. We must work hard to create and maintain harmony. That is not a natural state in the relative world. The natural tendency is towards chaos. This is a sad but true fact. We must not lay our heads down in defeat. We must remain positive and counterbalance with positive outcomes and projections.

Furthermore, with the knowledge of Pure Soul, we remain separate as knower-perceiver-seer. This does NOT mean we are indifferent. Actually, it is just the opposite. We validate and acknowledge all that occurs, we just do not endorse it with opinions. Our intention is to clear the outstanding balance. We want a resolution, not a pending claim in our files. We are not callous and unfeeling towards the afflictions, misery and pain in the world. Quite contrarily, our prayers are geared towards the betterment of the world. We pray for peace and joy throughout the world for all the people of the world.

We must hold a deep and profound compassion in our hearts for the people of this world especially the poor, underprivileged, abused and neglected ones. Ignorance is a serious torture that cannot be overcome without the guidance of one who is at a higher spiritual level. Our prayer is that no matter what race, creed or religion a person may be, that each and every person find a guide that is able to lead them to higher spiritual levels. Not everyone is ready for the Science of Absolutism. The Science of Absolutism is a system that has a set of tools enabling people to look within and better their lives inside and out. Everything starts on the inside. If there is a cancerous growth inside the body it is bound to show it's effects on the outside. The pain, misery, depression, and loss of hope that victims of cancer face are undisputed. Similarly, in a world of abundance and excess of every type of pleasure, there is a pain, anguish and hopelessness that runs deep within the veins and heart of many people. Let's spread the Science of Absolutism to help douse these fires.

Verse #103

"Engage in 'real' effort incessantly, do not fret about anything else; release the reigns to the energies of the impartial cosmic computer."

༄

Reflective Flashes—

Everything we actually try to 'do' is a waste of time! How scary! We are taught all our lives to 'do'. We must be natural and flowing in all our efforts and actions. It is without any pull, friction or effort that things should happen. When things occur naturally, the outcome is usually very positive. The 'real' effort is in remaining observer as Pure Soul, engaging in prayers upholding and elevating Pure Soul and being ever humble in the relative. THAT is 'real' effort. The relative life is not in our hands. When we truly come to that 'exact' realization our lives will take a true turn. The epiphany occurs when this is

'exactly' experienced. The 'exact' understanding of the energies of the impartial cosmic computer cannot take place until it is experienced. It is like riding a bike. We can read about it, we can talk about it, we can think about it, but until we actually DO it or experience what it is like, our knowledge of riding a bike is incomplete or partial.

It takes practice to be in 'real' effort. For infinite lives we have been accustomed to 'make believe' effort! The 'real' effort has never been known. We have never truly made any efforts! They were imagined or superimposed efforts. We took credit for effort that was not really our own! We made a habit of doing that! When things did not go our way, then we blamed it on someone or something else! We even blamed God infinite times out of our ignorance! We did not know we were condemning our very own being. What a crime! What a sickness. It is scary to imagine the implications of these karmas. We know the chaos that we face... the ignorant input that we had fed into the cosmic computer is the reason! We must keep smiling in the name of Pure Soul. Our joy should never be dampened. Our joy is 'real'. It is there whether the relative self (our neighbor and best friend) is smiling, laughing, crying, dancing, thinking, praying, studying, working, cooking, cleaning, complaining, sleeping or watching TV. 'We' remain in our Pure Soul as Pure Soul knowing and seeing everything as it is without any illusion. Rejoice as knower-perceiver-seer and allow our hearts to overflow with pure love and compassion for every living being. Trust me, people will feel it. Even the ignorant cannot ignore what their hearts feel.

Verse #104

"In the relative, engage in earnest and sincere relative effort, then release the reigns to the energies of the impartial cosmic computer; whatever has already transpired is exact destiny as ordained by the universal impartial cosmic computer."

ॐ

Reflective Flashes—

There is nothing that is carved in stone in our lives. We must be ready to change and transform at any given moment in the relative. Depending on the nature of our karma, our lives may even be seriously schizophrenic! Do not blame anyone if this is the case! It is our own doing. In this age of clash and conflict, we must be EVER ready to switch hats, learn a new song & dance, and even do things we vowed we would not ever go back to doing as far as work. Relative life has no guarantees. We must be sincere, make every effort to play our part, do our part and be successful at whatever we attempt in our lives. This is compulsory. We think that we chose to do this or that! No, it is compulsory. We superimpose the false ego that we made the choices. What if those choices were bad? Then, we blame someone, something or God for that! Is the utter ludicrousy of all this starting to become apparent? We must be 100% responsible for our own results. This is a given. We know in our hearts whether we have given it 110%, even in the relative. If we did not, then there could be a chance that the account remains pending. The thermometer is within. We KNOW. Be honest, earnest and sincere in all dealings in the relative. What are we taking with us to the grave? NOTHING. Our fragrance should linger long after we are united with mother earth. The fragrance of our character is what should be left behind, not demand notes in relative dealings!

The past is dead. It was actually divine truth. It happened so it is what it was. It was a result so it was justice as ordained by nature in all its infinite grace. There is no point in analyzing, crying over, pouring over, or even living in the memory of the past! The past is to be learned from. Whatever we remember is where our accounts are still unsettled. Neutralize those attachments and detachments from the past with 'real' effort. Pray, confess, repent and confirm that those mistakes will never be made again! Freedom reigns if we can become focused and present in both 'real' and 'relative'.

Verse #105

"You have come with everything you need, so put away the anxieties and tensions; time will unravel the inevitable undoubtedly and in perfect divine order."

ॐ

Reflective Flashes—

Our biggest obstacle to putting away the anxieties and tensions is our intellect! It drives us crazy. What if this happens? What if that does not happen? What about this? What about that? If we listen to our intellect, it can drive us nuts! We must keep intellect in its place. Our life is for the purpose of living a positive, productive, joyful, purposeful and healthy life without clash or conflict with any living being. We have our spiritual goals, material goals, career goals, personal fitness goals, family life goals and our personal relationship goals. It is great to have goals. It helps us to stay on track and keep perspective in these difficult times. However, we must NEVER engage in worry, anxiety or excessive stress. That is a waste of time and can actually keep us from progressing in every area of our life. The key is to be in motion at all times. If we are physically idle, there is no one to demand our mental, verbal or emotional energy, it is not time to be wasted! Be in motion in the 'real' effort. Engage in prayer, song, repentance, and reflection, reading Absolute Science books or other 'real' efforts that will build our balance for Pure Soul. If nothing else, we must practice 'seeing' Pure Soul in other living beings! It sounds a little nutty, but this is the way to maximize our human existence on this earth.

This science is to be fully understood and utilized to make our lives and the lives of others better. There is no repression, sublimation or depression involved with the Science of Absolutism.

The world is in divine order and always has been in divine order. The chaos and craziness is a result of our own projection of anger, pride, attachment and greed. Lechery has been rampant in this age. Therefore, we see and hear about the sick and stomach-turning things like rape, murder, and abuse. Where does the 'divine' order come in the picture with these 'sick' things? There is nothing divine about the 'sick' things. They are a result of human beings weaknesses. Nature must create what is wished, intended and projected by human beings.

We must live with courage and patience. The changes will come. It is up to those with Pure Soul in the palm of their hands to be divinely instrumental.

Verse #106

"The sounds that are made, accordingly the echoes will follow, understand this well; do not find fault with the echoes as they resonate with exact frequency and wavelength."

❧

Reflective Flashes—

It is a boomerang effect! If you shout into a canyon or well, 'I am an idiot,' that is what will come back at you ten fold! We project ourselves whether we say anything or not. The inner voice projects louder than anything! If we shouted into a well, 'I am a thief.' It will resonate back, 'I am a thief.' If we project 'I am Pure Soul,' then that is what will resonate back at us. Our inner attitudes and self-worth project what the world sees and hears. We can only fool ourselves. The world cannot be fooled! We may even be able to fool some people for a short amount of time, but eventually the truth reveals itself! In today's world, no one can pull one over on anyone. We are becoming more and more transparent!

Now, what we are hearing today is a result of what we shouted into the cosmic well in the past! We cannot cry about it or demand different. This is a result. We cannot change the result. We can however be vigilant and alert when feeding new sound waves into the cosmic well! The results of today should very well educate us on what we do NOT want to feed into the cosmic well. How flattering is it to be thought of as a cheat, liar or thief? When all that we aspire for is material wealth, fame and respect, this can happen! It really depends on how that material wealth, fame and respect is acquired. Today's wealth is not the highest quality wealth. It is not the fault of the money itself. It is the intentions behind the desire for the money. This is all money that is acquired without any respect, normality or positive contribution, therefore, leaves it mark by destroying families, marriages and communities. We, as human beings, have all the power!

Our intentions, deeds (both good and bad), aspirations, hopes, dreams and passions drive the cosmic computer to do its thing. Of course, there is always the natural justice that kicks in when there is excess. Excess is poison. For example, the excessive obsession and abnormality with sex has given rise to AIDS and sexually transmitted diseases.

Sounds are made with every breath that we breathe. It is very, very subtle and deep in concept. Be alert, be vigilant and accept your results.

Verse #107

"You have brought your account balances with you, for better or for worse it is your own fault; with calm serenity and equilibrium suck it up and live-out your life."

❧

Reflective Flashes—

Once you sign a contract there is no reneging on it! There are penalties for forfeiture. We signed, sealed and delivered the contract for this lifetime and dumped it into the cosmic computer for processing. This lifetime with all its quirks, adventures, triumphs, traumas, disappointments, heartbreaks, wonders and uniqueness is the result of that contract! This contract has no forfeiture clauses! The price must be paid no matter what! So, why not do it with a smiling face and twinkling eyes? It is, after all, our own creation! We all, as human beings, have the choice to an attitude. Attitude is really perception and vision as regulated by intellect. How do we see things? Do we constantly see the negative in all people and situations? Do we see the tiny spec of dirt on an otherwise sparkling clean floor? Do we always notice what is wrong with our children instead of seeing all the wonderful qualities and attributes they have? Are we overcritical of ourselves? When we look in the mirror, what do we see? Is there the face of a kind and loving person? Is there love and compassion in those eyes? Or is this person cold, unfeeling and devoid of positive feelings? Do we constantly criticize our loved ones? Are we defensive and are we controlling in our attitude? The sooner we are honest with ourselves the better.

After the Pure Soul is known, it is up to us to keep our neighbor or best friend in line. There is no excuse for a negative attitude! It is our job to keep our neighbor positive. We can occasionally give a pat on the shoulder, say a few kind words in the mirror to encourage or even just validate the trials and tribulations that are being faced on a daily basis. There is no harm in that. It is when the behavior and attitude of the relative self negatively impact others that are a problem. This is not acceptable! Through the complete understanding of the Science of Absolutism, it is possible to change those ingrained negative responses and attitudes. There is tremendous power in this science if used correctly and appropriately. The bottom line is you get what you give. It we do not give pain to any living being, we will be free from it! On the other side, we will find infinite joy and peace.

Verse #108

"You are 100% Pure Soul without a glimmer of doubt, forgetting your own 'Self' you buzz around; so, worship and praise the Pure Soul incessantly."

ॐ

Reflective Flashes—

It is so easy to get caught-up in the relative self and the paranoia that our neighbor has brought from infinite lives. The relative self is insecure and basically a victim of circumstances and the functioning of the cosmic computer. We must have unfettered compassion for our best friend, our neighbor. It is not easy to be a top spinning as ordained by nature's forces! We must console, appease, encourage, comfort and fill up the empty space in the heart of our best friend and neighbor for this lifetime. One of the greatest gifts we can give our best friend is to teach the worship and praise of the Pure Soul. It will function to soothe and comfort our neighbor and best friend. At the same time, will help us to reach our goal of freedom! In order to be free, we must clear this account with our best friend and neighbor. The accounts must be brought to a balance of zero at every level. In reality, our biggest account is with our neighbor and best friend. If we cannot keep our neighbor happy and healthy, our neighbor is unlikely to keep the rest of our files in order! It is a domino effect. If the CEO of the company does not gain the support of the Board of Directors, how can he/she be successful running the rest of the company? Until now, our false super-imposed ego was the CEO/President. There was nothing but chaos and confusion with that ruler. But now, Pure Soul is CEO/President. Things are different! Since the main culprit, ego, is in the right place, things fall into their appropriate places. The Pure Soul must make the Board of Directors (neighbor including intellect, ego, reflective mind and material mind) a complete and loyal ally. If this can be accomplished, half the battle has already been won!

How to make our best friend and neighbor our biggest cheerleader and ally? Treat them like a true best friend and neighbor should be treated. Be kind, honest, loving, compassionate and sincere in your dealings with your best friend and neighbor. Validate the grievances, heartaches and setbacks. However, at the same time, give firm direction and wise consultation. The Absolute Scientist has given us the keys to open any lock. We must wisely, prudently, appropriately and humbly utilize these keys to reach plateaus that we have never known both spiritually and in the relative world.

Nine Priceless Universal Prayers for Blissful and Peaceful Living

-Originally given by late Shri Dada Bhagavan in Gujarati
Originally translated by Mahatma and Professor Shri G. A. Shah

1. *Oh Pure Soul within every living being! May you bless me with such an infinite inner strength as would restrain me from hurting, causing someone to hurt or supporting someone hurting, even slightly, the ego of any living being.*

    May you bless me with such an infinite inner strength in the Philosophy of Relative Pluralism (Syad-Vad) in speech, conduct and thinking as would restrain me from hurting, causing someone to hurt, or supporting someone hurting, even slightly, the ego of any living being.

2. *Oh Pure Soul within every living being! May you bless me with such an infinite inner strength as would restrain me from hurting, causing someone to hurt or supporting someone hurting, even slightly, the authenticity of any religion.*

    May you bless me with such an infinite inner strength in the Philosophy of Relative Pluralism (Syad-Vad) in speech, conduct and thinking as would restrain me from hurting, causing someone to hurt, or supporting someone hurting, even slightly, the authenticity of any religion.

3. *Oh Pure Soul within every living being! May you bless me with such an infinite inner strength as would restrain me from enacting any verbal wrangle, misdeed, or misconduct to any living preacher, monk, nun or religious head.*

4. *Oh Pure Soul within every living being! May you bless me with such an infinite inner strength as would restrain me from enacting, causing someone to enact, or supporting someone enacting, even slightly, indifference to, or abhorrence for any living being.*

5. *Oh Pure Soul within every living being! May you bless me with such an infinite inner strength as would restrain me from speaking, causing someone to speak, or supporting someone speaking harsh and 'sticky' language to anyone.*

    May you bless me with an infinite inner strength of speaking soft and sweet language at all times, despite another's biting, bitter and scathing language.

6. *Oh Pure Soul within every living being! May you bless me with such an infinite inner strength as would restrain me from committing the carnal deeds, desires, or gestures, causing someone to commit them or supporting someone*

committing them to any living being, be they of any gender (masculine, feminine or neuter).

May you bless me with an infinite inner strength of keeping 'me' forever free from the cobweb of the Cupid!

7. *Oh Pure Soul within every living being! May your bless me with an infinite inner strength of controlling my temptation of regaling in any relish or flavor of food.*

May you bless me with an infinite inner strength in taking well-balanced, wholesome pure vegetarian food!

8. *Oh Pure Soul within every living being! May you bless me with such an infinite inner strength as would restrain me from enacting any verbal wrangle, misdeed or misconduct, causing someone to do so or supporting someone doing so, to any living being, directly or indirectly, living or dead.*

9. *Oh Pure Soul within every living being! May you bless me with an infinite inner strength for being instrumental in establishing 'real' well-being-ness in the world!*

Jay Sat Chit Anand!
Hail to the Bliss of the Alert Pure Soul!

What is the Science of Absolutism?
A Brief Overview

The Science of Absolutism is based on the fact that every living being has a relative self and a real self. The relative self is temporary and the real self is permanent. The relative self is super-imposed through false ego and the real self is pure. The relative self has a name and the real self is Pure Soul for each and every living being.

The Absolute Scientist (Gyani Purush) has the incredible power to draw the line of demarcation between the two: Relative Self and Real Self. The Absolute Scientist has been searching for infinite lives for a way to free people from the cycle of birth and death. His infinite search led to the master key enabling Him to separate the relative and the real. This requires the tremendous firepower of real knowledge. Due to the infinite layers of ignorance from infinite lives, His task is a daunting one. He accomplishes this in just one hour! Imagine the conditioning of infinite lives can be burned away to ashes in just one hour with the infinite firepower of real knowledge!

The purpose of the Science of Absolutism is to enable human beings to be freed from the endless cycle of birth and death. Also, to learn to live in peace, harmony and enjoy the inherent joy that is a part of being alive. We have lost that in translation in this age of chaos and conflict. What is truly of value is scorned upon and that which leads to death and destruction is envied and revered. What craziness have we come to? That which is pure and natural is considered boring. That which leads to disease, destruction, pain and sorrow is upheld and considered exciting. What is wrong with our world? Where did we go wrong? There has become gluttony of greed, lust and recklessness unequaled in any other age. Just like alcoholism, it becomes a vicious cycle. How to be free? How to rise above this? This is the ultimate dilemma.

The Science of Absolutism offers a true explanation of karma. How is it bound? It is bound through our intentions, not by our actions. This is very subtle yet crucial to our understanding of how the Science of Absolutism can enable us to attain permanent freedom from the cycle of birth and death.

The Science of Absolutism enables us to see life as it really is and not through the illusive perspective of our own anger, pride, attachment and greed. We are able to see things in their raw form whether from a relative standpoint or a real standpoint. The puzzle is solved when we can properly identify real and properly identify relative. When the understanding becomes crystal clear, so do the vision and the knowledge. The Science of Absolutism is a FACT. It cannot be disputed! It is a priceless and unequalled system for attaining eternal freedom.